Diversification Strategies for Regulated and Deregulated Industries

Diversification Strategies for Regulated and Deregulated Industries

Lessons from the Airlines

Jonathan L.S. Byrnes
Northeastern University

Lexington Books
D.C. Heath and Company/Lexington, Massachusetts/Toronto

387.7
B99d

Library of Congress Cataloging in Publication Data

Byrnes, Jonathan L. S.
  Diversification strategies for regulated and deregulated industries.

  Bibliography: p.
  Includes index.
  1. Air lines—United States—Management.   2. Diversification in industry—United
States.   3. Corporate planning—United States.   I. Title.
HE9803.A4B97   1985   387.7'068   83-48638
ISBN 0-669-07272-9 (alk. paper)

Published simultaneously in Canada
Printed in the United States of America on acid-free paper
International Standard Book Number: 0-669-07272-9
Library of Congress Catalog Card Number: 83-48638

To My Parents,
Sylvia and John Byrnes

Contents

Figures and Tables

Preface and Acknowledgments

Managing a regulated or newly deregulated company in the current era of change is a very difficult task. Deregulation is profoundly shifting the economic structure of many industries, and transformations of long-stable cost structures, demand trends, and technologies are altering the fundamentals of others. The airline, broadcasting, bus, financial services, moving, pipeline, public utility, oil and gas, railroad, telecommunications, trucking, and water transport industries are among those that have been significantly affected. To survive and to prosper, many managers in these industries are being forced to make fundamental changes in companies that have remained stable for many years. In doing so, they face a far more difficult management task than that of managers in traditionally competitive businesses.

Several diverse fields of study provide important insights into different aspects of this problem, including industrial organization economics, business policy, regulatory economics, competitive strategy, transportation and utility economics, and managerial economics. This book attempts to bring together the relevant portions of these disparate fields, apply them rigorously to the problem, and present them in a form that is pragmatically useful to the managers of these firms.

The research on which this book is based was conducted over several years. The initial portion was presented as as doctoral dissertation at the Harvard Graduate School of Business Administration in 1980. Work conducted since then has updated the material to cover deregulation more fully and has broadened the scope of the study to draw lessons for the managers in a range of regulated and newly deregulated industries. At all times, the research has attempted to focus on the pressing problems of the managers in the field.

Acknowledgments

I am grateful to many people who have made significant contributions to this study, particularly to the three members of my original Harvard thesis committee, who have provided substantial assistance and guidance for the original dissertation and for the substantial reorientation and further development that followed. John Meyer has been an invaluable source of insight and information on the airline industry and on regulation in general. As an advisor and teacher, he has provided a standard of excellence in scholarship and its application to important problems of business and government. His particular influence on the deregulation chapter of this book, which was extensive, is specifically acknowledged. Michael Porter has contributed an important perspective that combines business policy and industrial organization economics. The intraindustry competitive strategy sections of the book draw heavily on his pioneering work. I am also grateful for his assistance in working through the organization of this book and for his encouragement as I grappled with some of the more difficult issues. David Maister gave very helpful advice on the important day-to-day problems of research and presentation and on the strategic problems of research design and focus.

In addition, I am grateful to Roy Shapiro, also of the Harvard Business School, for reading and commenting on several sections of the manuscript, to Raymond Kinnunen of Northeastern University, for sharing his expertise on the financial services industry and for helping to refine many of my preliminary ideas, and to Heidi Vernon Wortzel, also of Northeastern University, for commenting insightfully on the entire manuscript.

Several current and former airline executives have been very helpful in discussing their respective firms and the industry in general. I wish to thank Rexford Bruno, Harry Mullikin, Lynn Himmelman, and Irwin Williamson of UAL; Wayne Hoffman, Thomas Grojean, Martin Lynch, Williams Evans, and Jackson Goss of Tiger International; Charles Simons of Eastern Airlines; Albert Casey of AMR; and several other executives who asked to remain anonymous. Also, I wish to thank James Barker of Moore McCormack Resources for sharing with me his views on transportation company diversification; Kirk Kramer of Temple, Barker and Sloane for his reflections on the telecommunications industry; and Richard Trask of Citibank for numerous insights into the airline and shipping industries. I am also grateful to Raphael Recanati and his management group for affording me an in-depth view of a major transportation company that is run with great effectiveness and integrity. John Schmidt of the Civil Aeronautics Board was very helpful in providing recent airline financial data.

I wish to thank the 1907 (UPS) Foundation, which has generously supported research in transportation and logistics, for funding the initial portion of this study, and the William B. Harding Foundation for the fellowship awarded me during the initial period of the study. I am also grateful to the Research and Scholarship Development Fund of Northeastern University for generous assistance in the later portion of the study. Dean Philip McDonald and Associate Dean Thomas Moore generously provided their understanding and additional support that helped in the preparation of this book. In addition, the resources and helpful staff of the Baker Library at Harvard Business School (particularly those in the Corporate Reports Department of the Cole Room) were crucial to this study.

Several individuals have contributed to my research effort and to my development. In particular, I am grateful to my Northeastern colleagues, Raymond Kinnunen, Robert Lieb, and Daniel McCarthy, for their guidance and support. James Heskett, D. Daryl Wyckoff, Jose Gomez-Ibanez, Robert Leone, and the late Raymond Bauer of the Harvard Business School, as well as James Baughman, now of General Electric Corporation, provided encouragement and instruction. Ernest Williams and Arthur Arsham of Columbia University and Henry Marcus of the Massachusetts Institute of Technology were instrumental in nurturing my interest in transportation and other regulated industries. My former Harvard and Columbia classmates and now colleagues, Jeanne Lynch, Frederick Hooper, Ivor Morgan, Norman Fast, Nitin Mehta, and Charles Davis, provided invaluable advice, assistance, and friendship throughout the study and manuscript preparation. I am also very grateful to my students, who helped clarify my ideas and who provided insightful feedback at every point.

I am particularly grateful to June Remington, who typed and revised numerous versions of the manuscript with prodigious speed and accuracy and astonishing good cheer. Sue Skalder and Sally Markham were also helpful at various stages in the preparation of the manuscript. Margaret Zusky and the staff of Lexington Books provided valuable assistance in the production of the book.

Finally, I would like to thank my wife, Marsha, and my sons, Daniel and Steven, for enduring the long work hours, lost weekends, and endless clutter that accompanied this work. My sister, Pamela, was also an important source of support and encouragement.

Although many individuals have contributed to this book, I accept full responsibility for all errors of commission and omission.

1
Introduction

As major sectors of the U.S. economy are increasingly deregulated, managers in both regulated and newly deregulated industries have sought a pragmatic framework for formulating their corporate strategies and for learning from the experiences of others. Regulation imposes a unique set of problems on businesses, and deregulation offers a new set of opportunities and dangers. Making the transition from regulation to deregulation is difficult, but it can be very rewarding. Many managers have tried to relate both their experiences under regulation and the experiences of other regulated firms to their prospects in a deregulated world so that they can retain what is useful and adjust where necessary. In working through their strategies, problems often have arisen in two areas: formulating a competitive strategy within the traditional industry and deciding on diversification into other industries. All too often, these two problem areas have been considered in isolation from each other and from other experiences under regulation.

This book develops a framework and systematic procedure for formulating corporate strategy that encompasses both intraindustry competitive dynamics and interindustry corporate diversification, and that can be applied in both regulated and deregulated contexts. To do this, the book focuses on corporate strategy broadly, as a multi-industry problem. At a very basic level, when managers ask themselves which business they are or should be in and what kind of company theirs is or should be, they are dealing with multi-industry issues and choices.[1] Because a company's prospects in its traditional business are a key component of the decision, however, a manager must start by analyzing the business's competitive dynamics and the company's relative position within that business. After that, one can move on to consider the relative merits of remaining solely in the business or moving partially or fully into others. The influence of economic regulation complicates the problem of analyzing intraindustry competitive dynamics.[2] But, while there are important differences among the various regulated and newly deregulated industries—in both the precise policies that regulators have used and the underlying industry economic structures—generalizations can be made to the extent that managers in all of these industries face the same analytical problems in the process of strategy formulation as well as many structural similarities. This multi-industry strategic perspective makes this book unusual among major studies of regulation and the transition to deregulation since the others tend to focus primarily on the single-industry regulated businesses.[3]

The strategic framework developed in the next section will be used to systematically analyze the dynamics of the airline industry over the past five decades. Many managers in regulated and newly deregulated businesses have looked to the airline industry for guidance in framing their corporate strategies; yet the experience of the U.S. airline industry, both under regulation and throughout its transition into deregulation, has seemed to be marked with turmoil. Stark contrasts characterized the industry under regulation: many of the nation's largest carriers were moving strongly into a variety of diversification ventures, ranging from hotels in exotic locations to insurance adjustment to fast-food chains, while most smaller carriers focused contentedly on their airline businesses year after year. The diversifying ventures themselves exhibited polar extremes in performance; some contributed handsome cash flows through thick and thin, while others failed to move out of the red. The changes under deregulation have also been extreme: several established firms are rapidly exiting the business, while others are prospering and still others have gone bankrupt. At the same time, several companies are shedding their subsidiary businesses, while others are accelerating them and moving into even newer fields.

By developing a general strategic framework and using it to analyze the airline industry, this book seeks to help managers in regulated and deregulated companies answer three specific sets of questions:

1. What is an appropriate corporate strategy for a regulated firm, and when is it advantageous to diversify?
2. How can firms best manage the transition into deregulation, and what role should diversification play?
3. What determines the success or failure of diversification ventures?

The first two questions concern strategy formulation, and the third concerns strategy implementation. A firm must do both well to succeed.

The strategic framework that follows will be useful for understanding the airline industry's experience. Next, an overview of the airline industry summarizes how this framework can be used in formulating strategy under both regulation and deregulation. The subsequent chapters present a focused industry study of airline corporate strategy spanning the industry's history. The final chapter fully develops a systematic procedure for deducing effective strategies, draws general conclusions for managers in the airline industry and other regulated and newly deregulated industries, and discusses the public policy implications of regulated and deregulated company diversification.

Strategic Framework

The airline industry's experience can be distilled into a strategic framework, which is a structure for understanding and relating the factors important to a company in formulating its strategy. This framework has direct usefulness for managers, as it can explain and predict an industry's successes and failures, and can be translated into a procedure that enables managers to deduce and evaluate explicit corporate strategies for their firms. In general terms, the airline experience strongly suggests that the formulation of corporate strategy should be a multilevel procedure. At one level, a company should set policies and programs that position the company within its traditional business; most managers tend to focus on strategy at this level. Yet at the same time it is crucial to broadly assess the company's prospects within its traditional business and to compare them to its prospective returns in others.

To judge its prospects in its traditional business, a firm must identify both its position relative to the basic competitive forces and dynamics of the business, and the industry's important environmental influences that will either help or hurt the company. A company's prospects within an industry are largely determined by five forces, identified by Porter (1980): the threat of new entrants, buyer bargaining power, supplier bargaining power, the threat of substitutes, and rivalry among existing firms. In the airline industry, for example, new airlines such as People Express are among the new entrants, business and pleasure passengers are among the buyers, labor and equipment manufacturers are among the suppliers, and telecommunications, buses, and automobiles are among the substitutes. Price or service competition are among the dimensions along which rivalry among existing firms can take place.

Regulation is generally accomplished through particular policies that act on each of these five forces. To formulate its strategy, a regulated firm must analyze its position in this artificial environment, and determine whether it can reposition itself to gain better returns. A regulated firm can either jockey within the prevailing rules, or work politically to change the rules. When it sees significant long-run opportunities or threats in the regulated business, it can alter its corporate strategy to shift resources into or out of the business to maintain long-run returns.[4]

Deregulation lifts the artificial influences that regulation places on an industry's structure, and recasts the competitive position of the industry's firms. Most deregulated firms must make major strategic adjustments. To determine an appropriate corporate strategy, a deregulated firm must first analyze its prospects in its traditional business. It can do this by: (1) untangling the effects of regulation on the five forces, in order to see which possible strategies will rest on defensible strengths appropriate for the new competitive environment; (2) identifying temporary factors (such as equipment supply constraints) that can prevent the firm from making the transition to any of the possible new strategies; (3) assessing its own resources and competitive position to evaluate which potential strategies are feasible; (4) projecting its competitors' likely positions; and (5) choosing the feasible strategy within the traditional business that best insulates it from direct competition and offers the best returns. After this, the firm can size up its prospects in the deregulated business. As the firm's prospects within the deregulated industry deteriorate or improve with deregulation, more or less diversification becomes advantageous.

Thus corporate strategy for both regulated and deregulated firms must encompass two interrelated factors: the intraindustry competitive positioning of a company's traditional business, and the interindustry allocation of resources as its traditional business prospects wax or wane. This is the essence of the strategic framework and the systematic strategy formulation procedure that the framework suggests. As the body of this book shows applying the strategic framework to a particular company or industry is a detailed but tractable task. Figures 1–1 and 1–2 represent the application of the strategic framework to the airline industry before and after deregulation, and illustrate the discussion in the following section.

Overview of Airline Corporate Strategy

The basic goal of the U.S. Civil Aeronautics Board (CAB) throughout the bulk of the airline industry's regulated years was to maximize service while keeping the firms in the industry financially healthy. As the industry evolved, cross-subsidy became the chief mechanism for achieving this end. As one airline executive put it: "The CAB gave out routes like they were handicapping horses."[5] This policy had identifiable political sources and important strategic implications. Through cross-subsidy, the CAB worked to divert returns earned on prime services, such as New York–Chicago and the transcontinental routes, into uneconomical but politically desirable goals, such as service on sparse marginal routes, maintenance of weaker carriers, and sizable labor settlements.

Implementing cross-subsidy required controlling the five forces that determined the performance of the firms in the industry. By keeping entry barriers high through certification controls, the CAB kept the number of marginal firms at a manageable level. It also used route acquisition and abandonment proceedings to create barriers to mobility and exit, which kept incumbent firms from competing away the lush sources of cross-subsidy and from shedding the money-losing services that were being supported. Through rate regulation, the CAB overrode the intrinsic bargaining power of buyers and certain suppliers. Cross-subsidy required keeping prices artificially high in prime services and artificially low in marginal services, despite the fact that the price-insensitive buyers on the prime services (such as frequent business passengers) had more intrinsic economic bargaining power than the price-sensitive buyers on marginal services (such as infrequent passengers in outlying regions). The CAB did this because the latter buyers had more political clout through the Congress. Similarly, labor unions (a key supplier) benefited from generous contracts—which were passed along through high prices to the ultimate customers—because they, too, had more political influence than intrinsic economic bargaining power.[6]

In the industry's formative years (through 1960), the CAB's policies worked relatively well. Because primary demand was steadily expanding and many customers were relatively price-insensitive, the industry prospered while service increased. As the industry matured in the late 1950s and early 1960s, however, the growth rate in demand slackened considerably and new customers became increasingly price-sensitive. Consequently, the industry's dynamic turned from a non-zero-sum game competition into a zero-sum game competition. In this watershed period, cross-subsidy began to cause systematic differentials between the smaller carriers' returns (recipients of cross-subsidy) and the larger carriers' returns (generators of cross-subsidy). This trend was obscured in the mid-1960s as newly developed jets radically decreased operating costs and led to a spurt in industry growth and returns (see table 1–1[7]).

During the brief period of jet-induced prosperity, the airlines turned toward a peculiar form of diversification as a form of intraindustry competition. Most carriers in this period entered the hotel business in key locations in attempts to establish or protect a "historical interest" in important destinations, thus meeting a CAB-articulated criterion for route awards (see table 1–2). The routes sought were prime, long-haul services (primarily transpacific), on which jet operation promised very high returns. Ironically, these diversifying ventures (referred to hereafter as Type I diversification) represented a basic commitment to the airline industry itself. The carriers were "playing the regulation game" by angling for routes with these largely unprofitable subsidiaries. Although, at the time, the airlines had no choice but to diversify in this way, the CAB's requirement for these ventures was wasteful, hurt the industry, and opened the door for later diversification of an entirely different sort—a movement by large carriers to deploy substan-

Figure 1–1. Airline Corporate Strategy under Regulation

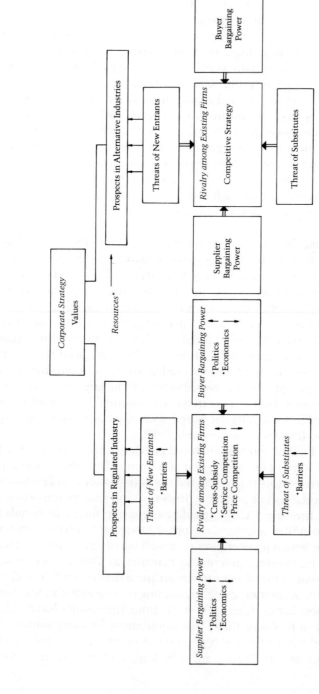

*Influenced by regulation; arrows indicate direction of influence.

Figure 1–2. Airline Corporate Strategy under Deregulation

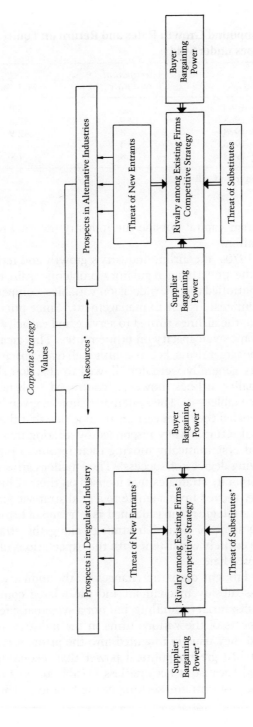

*Influenced by Deregulation.

Table 1–1
Average Compound Growth Rates and Return on Equity (ROE)
for All Airlines under Study

Period	Compound Growth Rate (%)	ROE (%)
1959–1963	8.3	5.8
1964–1968	12.9	17.3
1969–1973	7.8	2.9
1974–1978	9.0	6.7
1979–1983	7.8	(4.8)

Source: Derived from CAB data.

tial portions of their capital outside the industry (referred to hereafter as Type II diversification).

In the early 1970s, the airline industry's growth and returns declined dramatically as the underlying regulatory problems again took grip. Because the CAB controlled most key decision variables, competition became fierce along the dimensions left to management.[8] Since price competition was largely barred, the airlines turned to service and capacity competition, which led to chronic overcapacity on prime routes. This created a particular problem for the larger firms, because, although overcapacity drove down their returns, they generally were not allowed to abandon their marginal services. The smaller airlines, however, continued to benefit from protected services (see table 1–3). The systematic support given by the CAB to the smaller carriers led the larger carriers to conclude that they were facing chronic subnormal returns. They responded by altering their basic corporate strategies and systematically moving their resources into other businesses (with varying degrees of success). The smaller carriers largely continued parallel corporate strategies that focused on their airline operations. Thus, the industry moved from a single to a dual strategic group structure (see table 1–4). (A strategic group is defined as a "group of firms in an industry following the same or a similar strategy along the strategic dimensions."[9]) This was entirely consistent with the expectations of the strategic framework presented here.

Deregulation brought dramatic changes to the industry. Phasing out the artificial cross-subsidy mechanism and the related competitive constraints led to a substantial reshuffling, but not a systematic reversal, in the competitive prospects of the various firms in the industry. New entrants were allowed, and they usually migrated into the prime services. Labor, a key supplier that had greater political power than economic bargaining power, lost ground because it became less feasible to pass on high costs with the new low-cost entrants seeking prime business. The power posi-

Table 1–2
Overview of Air Carrier Diversification

Carrier	Subsidiary	Business	Started	Ended
American	Sky Chefs	Catering and in-flight services[a]	1942	—
	Americana Hotels	Hotels	1968	1979
	AA Energy and AA Development	Oil and gas	1976	—
	AA Training	Education	1979	—
Braniff	Braniff International Hotels	Hotels	1968	1982[b]
	Western Restaurants	Restaurants	1974	1977
	Braniff Educational Systems	Training	1972	1982
	Braniff International Resort Properties	Land development	1974	1982
Continental	Various hotels in Hawaii and Micronesia	Hotels	1967	1981[c]
Delta	None	—	—	—
Eastern	Hotels and land development in Hawaii and Puerto Rico	Hotels and land development	1967	1975
	National Distribution Services	Warehousing	1972	1975
National	None	—	—	—[d]
Northwest	Hotel in Japan	Hotels	1979	—
Trans World[e]	Hilton International	Hotels	1967	—
	Canteen Corporation	Catering and food services	1973	—
	Spartan Newfoods	Fast food	1979	—
	Century 21	Real estate brokerage	1979	—
UAL	Various hotels in Hawaii and San Francisco	Hotels	1968	1972
	Western International Hotels	Hotels	1970	—
	GAB Business Services	Insurance adjustment	1975	—

Table 1–2
Continued

Carrier	Subsidiary	Business	Started	Ended
Western	None	—	—	—
Pan American	Intercontinental Hotel Corporation	Hotels	1935	—
	Contract Services	Maintenance and operations	1950	1981
Tiger International	Tiger Leasing Group	Leasing	1970	1983
	Tiger Investors' Mortgage Insurance	Mortgage insurance	1976	1980
	Hall's Motor Transit	Trucking	1980	—
	Warren Transport	Trucking	1981	—
	Tiger Distribution	Distribution	1981	—

Source: Derived from SEC and annual reports.

[a] American is Sky Chef's largest customer.

[b] Braniff filed under Chapter 11 of the Bankruptcy Act in May 1982. It resumed operations in early 1984 with the backing of Chicago's Pritzker family.

[c] Texas International took over Continental in March 1982. Continental declared bankruptcy to reduce labor costs in September 1983 and quickly resumed operations.

[d] National was taken over by Pan American in January 1980.

[e] Trans World Corporation spun off the airline (TWA) during 1982 and 1983 after several takeover attempts.

Table 1–3
ROE Ranking by Strategic Group, 1969–1973

Group	ROE (%)
The Little Six	
Delta	14.6
Braniff	13.4
National	7.9
Northwest	7.9
Continental	5.7
Western	4.5
Mean	9.0
The Big Four	
United	4.8
Trans World	2.8
American	1.0
Eastern	(1.4)
Mean	1.8
Other	
Flying Tiger	19.6
Pan American	(7.3)

Source: Derived from CAB data.

Table 1–4
Maximum Proportions of Revenues Derived from Diversification

Group	Maximum Proportion (%)	Year
The Little Six		
Delta	0	—
National	0	—
Northwest	0	—
Western	0	—
Continental	0.8	1972–1975
Braniff	0.9	1975, 1976
The Big Four		
Eastern	1.8	1973, 1974
American	11.7	1973
United	12.0	1978
Trans World	35.0	1982[a]
Other		
Pan American	14.5	1979
Tiger	54.4	1980

Source: Derived from SEC and annual reports.
[a]The airline was spun off from the parent company in 1983.

tions of the two buyer groups were reversed: price-insensitive buyers—with substantial, real economic bargaining power—were better able to make deals with the companies competing for their business than were the infrequent marginal buyers. Interfirm rivalry became much more than a contest to curry favor from the regulators (through measures such as hotel siting) in an effort to gain more prime services and fewer marginal ones and much more than just a counterproductive, cutthroat capacity battle.

In the newly competitive, deregulated airline industry—as in other deregulated industries—a firm's prospects depended on its ability to formulate and implement a sound, defensible, competitive strategy that rested on strengths appropriate for the new environment. Firms could do this by developing individualized variants of three generic competitive strategies: (1) overall cost leadership, which centers on achieving low cost relative to competitors, usually through economical large-scale operations; (2) differentiation, whereby a firm creates a perception that it offers a unique product or service; and (3) focus, whereby a firm targets a specific set of buyers, a segment of the product line, or a geographic market.[10] The first two strategies are essentially market leadership strategies, and the third comprises a set of niche strategies. The particular competitive strategy a firm should pursue depends on its resources, its competitors' orientation, the underlying economic structure of the industry (as gauged by the aforementioned five forces), and its value system. Rarely, however, will a regulated company be well positioned to compete in a deregulated industry without some amount of fundamental repositioning.

Diversification should play a crucial role in mediating the transition from regulation to deregulation. By increasing or decreasing its diversification, a firm can tailor its traditional industry resources to the size necessary for its most appropriate competitive strategy (see figure 1–3). Large firms with basically strong intraindustry competitive postures generally should try to dominate the industry through market leadership strategies; alternatively, they should develop niches. In the former case they should draw on their diversification for resources (as necessary and available); in the latter case, they should increase it. Large firms with weak intraindustry competitive postures or depleted resources should retrench into defensible niches, strengthen their balance sheets, and increase their diversification—unless they can successfully perform the difficult task of strengthening themselves, perhaps drawing resources from their diversification, and moving toward market dominance.

Smaller firms with weak intraindustry competitive postures should migrate to profitable, defensible market niches, strengthen their balance sheets, and diversify with any remaining assets. Failing that, they should exit the industry entirely and diversify fully. Smaller firms with strong intraindustry competitive postures should either steadily build and develop

Figure 1–3. Transitional Strategies

	Large	Small
Strong	Likely: Build market leadership and divest diversification Alternative: Retrench to niche and diversify further	Steadily build niche and remain single-business
Weak	Likely: Retrench to niche and diversify further Alternative: Build market leadership and divest diversification	Retrench to niche (or exit) and diversify

Note: "Large," "small," "strong," and "weak" refer to a firm's status under regulation.

their niches or diversify with their remaining resources. (Although a new strategy should build on existing strengths and resources, firms too often simply try to jerry-rig strategies to fit the resources they carry forward from the earlier regulated era; chapter 5 gives several examples of this.) By following the strategy formulation process embodied in the strategic framework in this way, firms can move into profitable, defensible positions in a deregulated industry, adjusting their corporate strategies to maintain high overall returns. The industry itself will be transformed from a relatively simple single or dual-group structure to a more complex multigroup configuration.

The airlines had an opportunity to create specific, sound competitive strategies in several ways—notably, by (1) carving out relatively protected geographic market niches through strong hub or international gateway systems; (2) gaining market dominance through wide availability of high-quality service; (3) capturing the allegiance of particular groups of travelers; or (4) appealing to cost-conscious travelers with low fares based on low costs. Although some limited combinations were feasible, an airline that did not have a clear strategic focus faced difficulties. Because prior CAB regulation had favored airlines with high proportions of prime point-to-point routes serving high-density, price-insensitive customers, and because these routes were precisely the ones most exposed to competition from both low-cost-oriented new entrants and wide-service-oriented established firms with excess capacity, deregulation required that most airlines substantially alter their intraindustry competitive strategies and route structures. Doing nothing was the most hazardous transitional strategy.

Although steep fuel cost increases and recession have made the industry's deregulatory transition particularly tumultuous, several clear trends can be discerned. Four established airlines have been successful. Two large, strong carriers, United and American, have refocused their corporate strategies toward their airline businesses, as has Delta, a formerly small, single-business carrier that grew large and strong over the years. These firms have driven toward wide-service, market-leadership strategies resting on strong, multiple-hub route systems. Northwest, a smaller carrier with a strong, previously developed hub system and a low cost structure, steadily built on its strengths and remained focused on its airline business. In addition to these four, several new carriers successfully entered the business with sharply defined competitive strategies, and several regional and commuter airlines similarly prospered.

Several established airlines have been largely unsuccessful. Pan American and Eastern were large carriers that tried to remain relatively large wide-service firms but did not have the necessary resources and strong underlying multiple-hub or gateway systems to build upon. As a result of massive losses, Pan American was forced to retrench substantially, and Eastern may face this necessity. At the same time, Pan American was forced to sell its profitable nonairline subsidiaries to pay for its massive airline losses.

Western, Continental, and Braniff were small carriers that had problems because they continued to operate under the competitive assumptions that prevailed in the regulated era. Western and Continental remained small and carried a high proportion of prime, high-density, point-to-point routes that were vulnerable to competition. These carriers twice tried a merger, which the CAB disallowed and which would not have solved the underlying competitive problem. Ultimately, Continental was taken over by Texas International, an aggressive regional carrier, and Western remains very weakened by sustained massive losses. Braniff, the third carrier in this group, was a strong, smaller carrier that attempted to sprint to a market-leadership strategy without the strong multiple-hub system and resources that were necessary to support this strategy. It also did not have a benevolent CAB to provide a safety net, and it soon went bankrupt.

Trans World was a more complex case. Its airline was unsuccessful in achieving a wide-service strategy because it did not have a strong multiple-hub or gateway route system. Faced with mounting airline losses, a costly reequipment program, and periodic takeover attempts, the corporation downsized the airline into a niche player, spun it off, and became a very profitable nonairline conglomerate.

The difficulties sketched here suggest that the unsuccessful airlines ran into two sorts of problems. While the successful carriers built on strong competitive bases within the airline industry and the successful new entrants developed defensible niches, the unsuccessful carriers neither had nor developed defensible competitive postures within the airline industry. They did not have credible transitional strategies coupled with the necessary resources to implement them. Several of them largely ignored the fact that deregulation meant exposure on prime routes.

The second problem that many troubled carriers had in common was that they did not see the crucial role diversification could play in mediating the transition from regulation to deregulation. The successful diversified carriers refocused their resources, as needed, toward growth in their airline businesses.[11] This was largely a reversal of their Type II diversification and rested on the same economic principles. However, only one of the unsuccessful carriers, Trans World, retrenched its airline business and increased its high-performing diversification, while the others attempted to maintain their size or to grow larger in the airline business. Most of the firms ignored the alternative strategy suggested by the strategic framework, which was to define a defensible, high-return, competitive niche; to restructure; and, if necessary, to downsize into the niche and diversify any excess resources into other businesses. The amount of diversification then would have been related to their prospects in the airline industry, which, in turn, would have been related to the amount of resources needed to fill the feasible niches. Their multi-industry corporate strategies would have grown sensibly out of their intraindustry competitive strategies, and a new wave of Type II diversification would have emerged.

Four important factors slowed the pace at which the established airlines adjusted to deregulation, giving a temporary, but important, edge to new entrants. First, most established carriers' labor unions had long-term contracts and a substantial degree of residual political leverage. Wages fell only when new, low-cost entrants made significant inroads and several heavily unionized incumbent firms faltered. Similarly, the marginal buyers used their remaining political clout to slow price rises and abandonment. Second, as new types of equipment, such as fuel-efficient, short-haul aircraft, were required for the new strategies, backlogs in equipment manufacture and tight markets impeded the transition.[12] Third, lack of available gate space slowed route restructuring.[13] Finally, at times, the incumbent managements' values and orientation blocked the transition on two levels. Several carriers' management teams were not geared up for the fast-moving, competitive, deregulated industry and thus failed either to change strategies aggressively or to implement new ones aggressively. At the same time, several carriers' management teams seemed to view diversification as evidence of failure in the traditional industry or simply as alien to their business. In most cases, falling returns ultimately led to a change in management, but the delays severely drained resources and foreclosed choice niches.

For diversification to provide an attractive alternative to marginal opportunities in the traditional business, the ventures must provide high returns. The airlines have had very mixed results with their nonairline subsidiaries (see table 1–5). The ancillary but very important issue of what determined the success or failure of these ventures is analyzed at length in chapter 7.[14]

Methodology

Central to this book is a focused industry study of the U.S. trunk air carrier industry. The primary firms under study are traditionally divided into two groups: (1) the Big Four carriers—AMR (American), Eastern, Trans World (TWA), and UAL (United); and (2) the Little Six—Braniff, Continental,

Table 1–5
Comparison of Nonairline Businesses, 1972–1978

Business	*ROE[a] (%)*
Trans World: Hilton	28
Tiger: Leasing	18
Trans World: Canteen	15
Tiger: Insurance	14
Pan American: Intercontinental	11
UAL: Westin	8
American: Subsidiaries	4[b]
UAL: GAB Business Services	1
Braniff: Educational Systems	0
Braniff: Hotels	(21)
Eastern: Hotels	(36)
Eastern: Distribution	(37)
American: Hotels	Very low[b]
Continental: Hotels	Very low[c]

Source: Derived from SEC and annual reports.

[a]Some ROEs have been adjusted to achieve accounting consistency for comparison.

[b]Artificial figure, including substantial sales by Sky Chef to American. During this period, Sky Chefs reported aggregate gains of $39 million, and Americana reported aggregate losses of $19 million.

[c]During this period, Continental's hotels reported aggregated *losses* of $5 million.

Delta, National, Northwest, and Western. In addition, Pan American, a large international carrier, and Tiger International (Flying Tiger), a large all-cargo carrier, are included because they are important and have interesting diversification. Several newer and regional carriers are discussed in the deregulation section.

This industry yields particularly useful insights into the relationship between regulation and corporate strategy for several reasons. First, it was heavily regulated in both routes and rates for many years, and systematic differences in performance can be observed among firms within the industry. Second, recent deregulation has reversed the regulatory environment and has substantially altered the pattern of profitability. Third, there is a wide range in the degree to which these firms have diversified. Fourth, the firms that have diversified have undertaken both related and unrelated ventures, which have displayed a wide range of performance.

This study utilized a combination of statistical and clinical (interview) research methods. Where possible, the causes of carrier actions are inferred from CAB and SEC data; for example, a thirty-year series of CAB and SEC statistics on each firm has been examined to establish an association between air carrier profitability and diversification. At times, however, particular micro-level problems, such as airline-hotel strategy coordination, required interview data. By blending these diverse research methods, the study attempted to fashion a fuller understanding of the industry.

Synopses of Chapters

The chapters that follow develop and support the lines of argument summarized in this chapter. The strategic framework is used to analyze the airline industry and to suggest more general lessons for managers in this and other regulated and deregulated industries.

Chapter 2 traces the evolution of CAB regulation and shows how key policies developed. The important strategic groups, which grew out of the differential impact of regulation, had their roots in the early years discussed in this chapter. An understanding of this development sets the stage for the analysis of the pattern of corporate strategy that followed.

Type I diversification is the subject of chapter 3. This strategic movement, which took place in the late 1960s, grew out of the regulatory requirements of the time. Chapter 3 builds on the preceding chapter by showing how the particular regulatory mechanisms that had evolved induced most companies to adopt the particular diversification strategies of this period.

Chapter 4 analyzes the Type II resource allocation diversification that followed in the 1970s. This discussion traces the evolution of the industry's key strategic groups in the mature regulatory period and systematically links them to both regulation and diversification.

Chapter 5 continues the analysis by considering the industry's response to deregulation and how the firms managed the transition. It discusses deregulation's recasting of the strategic groups and creation of new opportunities and dangers.

Chapter 6 explores and analyzes a variety of alternative, or secondary, goals of corporate diversification. Enhanced utilization of tax benefits, reduction of cyclicality, financial speculation, joint operating or marketing economies, tying up of scarce resources, and selling of joint products or by-products are considered in turn and are assessed in light of the industry's actual experience.

The striking pattern of success and failure of diversification ventures is analyzed in chapter 7. Several possible factors are considered: relatedness to the main line of business; internal development versus acquisition; and internal exchanges between the venture and the airline. The industry's experience strongly suggests a rather surprising but logical conclusion.

The final chapter, chapter 8, draws more general conclusions and shows how to apply the findings to other industries. The results of the study are summarized and are used to confirm the usefulness of the strategic framework as a basis for normative presciptions for corporate strategies. The chapter also articulates the roles that competitive strategy and diversification can play in both regulated and deregulated firms, explores how best to diversify to achieve successful results, and assesses the impact of regulated and deregulated company diversification on society.

It is hoped that this book will enable managers in both regulated and deregulated industries to chart insightful strategies that will move their companies through a turbulent period and into a prosperous future.

Notes

1. See Andrews (1980); see also Christenson et al. (1982). Some companies look at corporate strategy as only an intraindustry problem. In many of these cases they are being overly narrow; by ignoring interindustry alternatives, they may be heading very efficiently into a dead end. It is necessary to look at a second level of corporate strategy.

2. Throughout this book, *regulation* will be used to refer to economic regulation as opposed to other forms of regulation, such as safety.

3. Meyer and Oster (1981, pp. 91, 92) provide an excellent analysis of airline deregulation, specifying that it is a single-industry study.

Early studies of regulation focused on describing the regulatory process. The focus shifted when Meyer et al. (1959) pioneered a prescriptive analytical study of the efficiency of federal regulation of the transportation industries. Caves (1962) further developed the industry study approach to the analysis of regulation. He compared a theoretically constructed model of how the U.S. air carrier industry would behave in the absence of regulation to the existing regulated industry and drew conclusions regarding the ideal form of regulation.

More recent studies have focused on the effects of regulation on particular aspects of the behavior of firms. Capron (1971), Maister (1978), and others have examined the role of regulation in inhibiting technical and organizational change in regulated industries. Averich and Johnson (1962) and others have examined the effect of rate-of-return regulation on the mix of factor inputs of the firm, predicting that capital intensity would result. Kahn (1970) summarizes a variety of similar effects. The common thread running through these studies is a focus on the effects of regulation on single-business firms.

Recently, however, many regulated firms, as well as many unregulated firms, have diversified out of their traditional main businesses into other ventures. This trend came sharply to the public's attention when the somewhat diversified Penn Central Railroad went bankrupt in 1970 (see, for example, Daughen and Binzen, 1973; U.S. Senate, Committee on Commerce, 1972). This led the ICC and the Congress to initiate a series of hearings on railroad diversification (U.S. Interstate Commerce Commission, 1977; U.S. Senate, Committee on Commerce, 1972). By the early 1970s, several air carriers had reorganized into holding companies and had undertaken a variety of diversification programs. The CAB held a series of hearings on this activity in the mid-1970s. (These hearings were conducted as the Air Carrier Reorganization Investigation, Docket 24283 et al.; key documents were U.S. Civil Aeronautics Board, 1973; U.S. Department of Transportation, 1973a, 1973b, 1973c, 1973d.) To date, however, the literature on multi-industry corporate strategies of regulated firms is exceedingly sparse. Cunningham and Wood, 1984 is a noteworthy exception; the study described in this book, much of which originally appeared in Byrnes (1980), was conducted completely independently and differs substantially from theirs.

4. Theoretically, a strong argument could be made for returning the excess resources to the stockholders, who would invest in a way that would maximize their utility. In practice, however, corporate managers do not readily give up control over substantial blocks of assets.

5. Simons interview (1979).

6. Labor unions have tight seniority and membership policies that insulate their members from the threat of new entrants, and they have strict work rules that protect them from substitutes such as capital (in the form of automation).

7. This table (and most others throughout the book) refers to the U.S. trunk airline industry plus two large important carriers with interesting diversification. See the methodology section of this chapter.

8. See Fruhan (1972); see also chapter 3 *infra*.

9. See Porter (1980, p. 129).

10. Porter (1980, ch. 2) discusses these generic competitive strategies in detail. Meyer (1983) has adapted Porter's (1980) discussion to the airline industry (see chapter 5 *infra*, note 24).

11. UAL delayed shedding its diversification because it had enough resources for the airline's growth and because of personal loyalties. Simon (1957) and Bower

(1970) cite organizational momentum, personal loyalties, and the risk that the change would not be permanent as factors inducing delay in response.

12. See Meyer and Oster (forthcoming-b); see also chapter 5 *infra*, note 20.

13. See Meyer and Oster (forthcoming-a).

14. Researchers who have studied the phenomenon of diversification have approached it either on a time-series basis, constructing growth models of firms, or on a cross-sectional basis, comparing the performance of a sample of firms that are pursuing different strategies of diversification. Chandler (1962) saw a discernible growth cycle that most older industrial firms had in common. He saw diversification as a response to a profit or growth crisis in the traditional product line. Chandler concluded that the direction and degree of diversification are determined by the range of application of the resources—that is, the sources of strength of the firm. He implied that firms prosper under related diversification because they can apply their special competences. Unrelated diversification was seen as the residual strategy. Chandler cited W.R. Grace, in particular, as having no transferable skills because it was in transportation, and he concluded that this problem led Grace into unrelated diversification—investing in businesses "largely as a Wall Street investment house" (p. 392).

Rumelt (1974) did the most thorough recent cross-sectional study of diversification. He classified a sample of 246 large U.S. industrial firms in 1949, 1959, and 1969 into categories that attempted to capture the spirit of the business policy model (as articulated by Andrews, 1971, and others), which predicts gains from building on strengths. Rumelt found that firms with related businesses performed best; single-business firms and conglomerates performed modestly; and unrelated-business firms (that is, firms with a dominant product and unrelated diversification) performed poorly. Rumelt lost all of the significance of the strategy-related variables, however, when he added a variable for industrial concentration (pp. 100–101). This suggests that, in addition to the proposition that acquisitions aimed at market control should do well, the industry structure alone was adequate to account for the performance of firms in his interindustry sample. Hence, his findings shed no light on performance differences among the firms in respective industries. Seen thus, one would expect that firms in high-performing industries would be better off diversifying into related products to fill out their product lines; and firms in poorly performing industries might be best off either maximizing their payout, given sunk costs and low marginal costs, or diversifying into unrelated fields. In the former case, modest earnings might mask high cash flows; in the latter case, aggregate performance might be pulled down by the poorly performing base industry, even if the unrelated businesses were doing very well.

2
The Early Years: 1934–1960

The airline industry's early years were marked by industry growth and evolving CAB regulation. As the industry moved toward self-sufficiency, regulatory policies that had been developed earlier to foster a weak fledgling industry became increasingly problematic and counterproductive. Yet a combination of complex political interactions and organizational momentum kept these policies in force. These problems led to the formation of strategic groups and, ultimately, to corporate strategies that shifted capital out of the business. A discussion of the development of regulation and its effect on firms in the industry through 1960 will provide the background necessary for understanding the competitive response that followed.

During the early years, two airlines developed businesses that looked like diversification but were actually part of their airline operations. Pan American's initial development of the Intercontinental Hotel chain in 1935 provided a needed service to the airline. In those days, transpacific and other long-distance flights took several days and required overnight stops. Pan American sited hotels where they had overnight stops and no accommodations were available.[1] Several years later, they also began doing minor contract maintenance for other carriers. American Airlines initially developed Sky Chefs in 1942 to cater its airline; for historical and other reasons (to be discussed later) it has remained a separate company. Thus, in the early years, all carriers were really single-business firms.

The CAB was established by the Congress in 1938. The enabling legislation, the Civil Aeronautics Act of 1938 charged the CAB with promotion and regulation of the air transport industry in pursuance of multiple objectives: to achieve the highest degree of safety; to maintain carriers in a sound economic condition; and to adapt the air transport system properly to the needs of the foreign and domestic commerce of the United States, the U.S. Post Office Department, and the U.S. military services. This mandate required that the CAB simultaneously maximize a set of objectives that probably could not be jointly maximized (for example, better economic conditions of carriers versus more safety).[2]

The conflicting set of objectives with which the Act charged the CAB reflected the politics of its birth. The Act was necessitated by the inadequacy of its predecessor, the Air Mail Act of 1934. The 1934 Act provided for tripartite control over the fledgling air transport industry. Since the prime commercial task of the industry at that time was carrying air mail, the Post Office Department determined routes and schedules. Although the Post Office Department awarded routes by having carriers bid competitively for one-year contracts, the veteran Interstate Commerce Commission set rates on the awarded routes for the succeeding years, and the Department of Commerce was given control over equipment specification. This system had a built-in problem of overlapping jurisdiction: to get route awards, carriers generally submitted unreasonably low bids to the Post Office Department for first-year service and later had the rates raised by the Interstate Commerce Commission. When it became evident that the system was unworkable, the Congress favored the recommendation of the Federal Aviation Commission that all regulatory powers be concentrated in one agency. A political struggle ensued in which the executive departments froze out the Interstate Commerce Commission and midwived an act that embodied the many objectives of the parties, rather than sorting them out.[3]

The policies of the CAB in its early years show the ongoing interaction between the political environment and CAB policymaking. In the years immediately preceding World War II, the air carriers depended almost entirely on air mail subsidies for revenues. They pressed for expanded routes, since this was the only way to increase their dollar inflow. This expansion was opposed by a political bloc composed of the House Appropriations Committee, the Department of Commerce, and the Post Office Department, which were against increased subsidies. The CAB stance in the prewar period was essentially conservative: the ultimate test of any proposed policy or ruling was its impact on the prevailing level of subsidy. The main CAB policies that emerged in this period—limited competitive route awards, a bar to new entrants, and a refusal to reduce fares—reflected this goal.[4] These policies were carried forward through the years and became important influences on the industry's internal competitive dynamics.

The World War II years were strong ones for air carriers. Demand increased, supply was limited, and, consequently, load factors rose. The CAB reacted by reducing fares and awarding new competitive routes to divert carrier earnings into increased service while maintaining existing subsidy levels. This policy was destined to run into trouble, because it was based more on past performance than on future conditions. The postwar market downturn realized the potential problems when war-related demand remained high but supply increased more rapidly, nonscheduled air carriers with war-surplus equipment moved into the lower end of the market, and the concurrent breaking in of new equipment resulted in several crashes and abnormally high costs. These problems led to a dramatic decline in carrier earnings and a dramatic increase in subsidy requirements.[5]

The substantial postwar increase in carrier subsidy requirements upset the political equilibrium, and a tumultuous adjustment process ensued. The House Committee on Interstate Commerce voiced the complaints of the nonairline segments of the transport industry that the air carriers were receiving excessive subsidies, while the Department of Commerce, reflecting its historic concern with safety in air transport, reasoned that the CAB had "overexpanded" the industry and blamed the CAB for the crashes. In 1947, a Presidential Air Policy Commission determined that air subsidies were too high; and during 1948, congressional pressure built to reduce the subsidies.

The CAB reacted by doing everything it could to raise the net earnings of the industry. It approved a general fare increase—a decision made with little knowledge of the probable effects. It also approved carrier experiments with off-peak fare reductions and a limited form of coach service, but it soon reversed itself for fear that the effective price decrease might lead to a revenue loss because of peak-to-off-peak and class switching. The CAB also reacted by pressuring the nonscheduled air carriers—because they were not easily controlled but were easily squeezed out and because, in fact, they were operating as trunk carriers (providing scheduled service even though they were not certified to do so). The underlying logic of these moves was to alleviate political pressure by reducing the subsidy level. To do this, the CAB attempted to keep the profits of trunk carriers up in good markets by keeping fares high and competition out so that the trunks would remain able to cross-subsidize their thin routes.[6] These policies, which further raised entry barriers and cross-subsidy, have been carried forward through the years.

The revised CAB policies aimed at subsidy reduction were rendered obsolete by the industry prosperity resulting from the Korean War. In 1950, profits of the trunk carriers rose substantially. Consequently, the antisubsidy pressure eased and an opposing political force favoring small business stepped up pressure on the CAB to increase the role of the nonscheduled air carriers. The Senate Select Committee on Small Business (responding to the pressure of noncertified carriers), the Department of Defense (a user of nonscheduled charter aircraft), and the Department of Justice (an advocate for competition) led the pro–small business forces. Mindful of the subsidy-level constraint, the CAB reacted to this pressure by finding in the landmark 1951 Southern Service to the West case that service at reduced prices was a good idea but that certified carriers could do the job by expanding reduced-rate coach service, effectively allowing fares to fall. This decision deflected some political pressure. It also enabled the CAB to retain control over the subsidy level, since the fare-reducing services could be canceled in the event of a recession, leaving the CAB with no new carriers to support in lean times.[7] Thus, the postwar struggle between the antisubsidy group and the pro-small business group was resolved with a compromise that reinforced the formidable regulatory barriers to entry developing in the business.

A profit downturn in 1952 led the carriers to ask the CAB for a fare increase. Not wanting to upset the political equilibrium developed in the Southern Service to the West case, the CAB slowly initiated a general fare investigation. When earnings returned to normal in 1953, the carriers pressed the CAB to drop the general fare investigation, fearing that the upturn would lead to a finding for fare reductions. In dismissing the investigation, the CAB noted that, despite fluctuations, carrier earnings over the period 1938–1952 were reasonable, and it formulated the "good years and bad" rule. This rule called for fare adjustments only if earnings were below the level necessary to provide a fair return over a reasonably extended period. The effect of this rule was to insulate the CAB from temporary disequilibrating pressures stemming from short-term economic trends. The pragmatic utility of this rule was borne out in 1954 when a minor recession brought carrier pressure for a fare increase, to which the CAB responded that the losses were only short-term. Indeed, in 1955, the industry recovered its losses and earned high profits.[8]

The mid-1950s saw the political ground shift under the carefully constructed CAB policy. The budget-balancing Eisenhower administration exerted considerable pressure on the CAB to reduce subsidies to air carriers. By this time, primary demand for passenger air service had expanded considerably, and carriers were earning high profits on many of their better routes. The CAB reacted by transferring good routes from some local carriers to trunks to wean the trunk carriers off subsidy.

By 1955, however, the pressure for budget balancing was eased, and the local carriers pressed for increased authority. Championed by the Senate Committee on Foreign and Interstate Commerce, the local carriers won from the CAB permanent certification, route extensions, and an implicit commitment for ongoing subsidies. By 1959, the congressional commerce committees had pressed the CAB into expanding the routes of local carriers so substantially that the House Appropriations Committee had to intervene by cutting the supplemental appropriations for their subsidies.[9]

Although the Congress gave a clear green light to subsidization of local carriers, the CAB continued to regulate trunk carriers by its old standards. Keeping them off subsidy was the dominant goal, and gaining improved service with any excess profits was the secondary goal. The high profits earned by the trunks in the early 1950s were not uniformly distributed among the carriers. The CAB, in a historically crucial move, adapted its subsidy-minimization policy to favor weaker trunk carriers in an effort to reduce the risk of having to subsidize an unprofitable trunk carrier.[10]

In this period, the CAB developed several policies aimed at shoring up weak carriers. Whereas noncompetitive route extensions into thin markets usually were awarded to local carriers at the behest of the Congress, route extensions into lucrative markets that the CAB deemed underdeveloped or underserviced by particular strong trunk carriers generally were awarded to the weaker trunks. This arrangement was not uniformly applied however; the CAB did not allow strong trunk carriers to move in on weak carriers in the weak carriers' best markets for fear that a profit reduction would lead to subsidies. In general, strengthening smaller trunk carriers took precedence over improving service as a CAB goal.[11]

The CAB also based its policy toward innovative trunk carrier fares and services in this period on a double standard that reflected its desire to support weak carriers. (Moreover, this policy was applied incrementally, which probably reflected the CAB's sensitivity to fare reductions, which had led in the past to subsidy problems.) The CAB often allowed weak carriers to experiment with new off-peak fares and coach services, but the tariffs generally were granted on a temporary and experimental basis, with various other goals (for example, extension of service) cited to justify the moves. The profitability of each arrangement was tested periodically under the rubric of "reasonableness."

In 1956, Representative Emanuel Celler's Antimonopoly Subcommittee of the House Judiciary Committee held a stormy series of hearings into the relationship between the CAB and the airlines. This affected CAB policy toward fare levels and, more important, toward carrier participation in the policy formulation process. The focus of the hearings was the CAB's dropping of the 1952 general fare investigation at the air carrier's behest, but the scope of the hearings spanned all carrier trade association activities and CAB rate setting. The political pressure generated by the Celler committee led the CAB to curtail carrier association participation in fare level hearings and to reinstitute a general fare investigation. The investigation, completed in 1960, found that the historical 10 percent long-term rate of return earned by carriers was acceptable. No standards were set, however, for future fare levels; that is, no way was sought to relate legal fares to past or present data. Thus, the CAB remained tied to hindsight regulation, awarding fare increases to carriers when their past-period profits dipped. This finding was destined to exacerbate carrier cyclicality, yet it was very consistent with the CAB's historical fear of seeing low rates of return lead to politically unacceptable subsidy levels.[12]

Thus, CAB regulation had been successful in nurturing carrier development in the industry's formative years by eliminating fare competition, by erecting barriers to entry into the industry and into city-pair market segments, and by selective subsidization. As the industry developed, the political pressure placed on the CAB in the 1950s became rather schizophrenic: in good years, there was pressure to certify marginal carriers; in lean years, there was pressure to minimize subsidies. In response to the former pressure, the CAB limited the number of carriers and enabled them to make substantial profits in strong markets, but it forced them to cross-subsidize thin routes and expand service to the public (thus obviating the need for new marginal carriers). In response to the latter pressure, the CAB periodically allowed weaker trunk carriers to enter the stronger carriers' better routes. Since CAB rate making and route granting were backward-looking, competitive route awards that seemed sensible at the peak of a cycle (looking backward at rising earnings) turned out to be disastrous during the downturn.

The CAB was able to maintain this balance while the industry was in its development stage (through the late 1950s), because the high overall growth and returns available in the industry kept even strong carriers focused on their airline opportunities. As table 2–1 shows, however, overall returns and growth were slowing by the late 1950s. Moreover, the four-firm concentration ratio (C4), a measure of the proportion of industry revenues captured by the four largest firms, declined significantly. This measure highlights the substantial effect of the CAB's cross-subsidy policy on the dominant carriers. The following chapters document in detail the competitive dynamics spawned by the systematic differential impact of the CAB's regulatory policies and analyze their effect on the corporate strategies of the firms in the industry.

Table 2–1
Performance of All Carriers under Study, 1951–1959

Year	ROE (%)	Growth Rate (%)	C4[a]
1951	11	12	.60
1952	13	12	.60
1953	11	13	.59
1954	12	11	.61
1955	12	15	.60
1956	12	14	.59
1957	7	10	.56
1958	7	6	.57
1959	9	17	.55

Source: Derived from CAB data.

[a]C4 = the four-firm concentration ratio, a measure of the proportion of industry revenues captured by the four largest firms.

Notes

1. See Davies (1967).
2. See Caves (1962, pp. 127–133).
3. Ibid.
4. See Caves (1962, pp. 142–147).
5. Ibid.
6. Ibid.
7. See Caves (1962, pp. 193–231).
8. Ibid.
9. See Caves (1962, pp. 280–299).
10. Ibid.
11. Ibid.
12. See Caves (1962, p. 287).

3
Playing the Regulatory Game: Type I Diversification

The steep earnings decline experienced by the airline industry in the late 1950s extended into the early 1960s, spanning the years 1957–1963 (see table 3–1). This reflected underlying problems rooted in the fact that the CAB's regulatory policies, which were designed to nurture an infant industry, were becoming increasingly inappropriate for a maturing industry. By this time, CAB regulation had led to severe cyclicality, to systematically higher small-carrier returns, and to a steadily eroding large-carrier market share (as measured by C4; see table 3–2). During the mid-1960s, the industry prospered, as newly introduced jet equipment drove down costs more rapidly than fares. This temporarily obscured the industry's fundamental regulatory problems.

By 1968, the carriers had reequipped, and a fierce, regulation-induced competitive struggle took grip. Regulation had channeled carrier competition into the few narrow areas, over which the carriers' managements had control, and cutthroat competition ensued along these dimensions. Carriers bought new types of equipment and increased schedule frequencies until they used up their resources. They also angled for regulatory favors, such as prime route awards. Type I diversification was an integral part of this competition. It grew out of a particular set of regulatory policies that the CAB itself later largely ignored in its route awards but that nevertheless shaped the industry's competitive dynamics. This diversification served little useful purpose, either for the carriers or for society as a whole.

CAB Regulation

The crucial role CAB regulation played in determining airline profitability in this period has been documented by Fruhan (1972). This documentation provides a basis for explaining the carriers' behavior in this period. Fruhan divided the set of determinants of air carrier relative profitability into those that were controlled by the CAB and those that were controlled by carriers' managements.[1] He then regressed these independent variables (plus a dummy variable for "firm effects") on a dependent variable representing the

Table 3–1
Summary Statistics of All Carriers under Study, 1960–1969

Year	ROE (%)	Growth Rate (%)	C4[a]
1960	5	10	.57
1961	(2)	7	.59
1962	8	14	.59
1963	9	26	.59
1964	17	13	.58
1965	23	17	.57
1966	18	15	.55
1967	20	21	.56
1968	9	12	.55
1969	6	11	.52

Source: Derived from CAB data.

[a]C4 = the four-firm concentration ratio, a measure of the proportion of industry revenues captured by the four largest firms.

Table 3–2
Performance Ranking by Strategic Group, 1959–1968

1959–1963		1964–1968	
Group	ROE (%)	Group	ROE (%)
The Little Six		*The Little Six*	
Western	13.3	Delta	23.8
Delta	12.8	National	22.4
National	11.9	Northwest	22.4
Northwest	9.8	Continental	20.6
Continental	8.0	Western	17.6
Braniff	4.3	Braniff	9.0
Mean	10.0	Mean	19.3
The Big Four		*The Big Four*	
American	8.6	American	15.9
United	5.9	Trans World	15.8
Trans World	2.3	United	11.5
Eastern	(19.1)	Eastern	5.0
Mean	(0.6)	Mean	12.0
Other		*Other*	
Flying Tiger	(3.3)	Flying Tiger	11.7
Pan American	9.0	Pan American	1.6

Source: Derived from CAB data.

relative profitability of the eleven domestic trunk carriers for 1955 through 1965. The carriers were divided into two groups: the Big Four—American, Eastern, Trans World, and United; and the Little Seven—Braniff, Continental, Delta, National, Northeast, and Western.[2]

Table 3–3 shows the overwhelming importance of CAB regulation in determining the air carriers' returns. For the Big Four carrier group, CAB-controlled variables were significant, explaining 84 percent of the observed relative profitability, whereas management-controlled variables were not significant at the $F.05$ level. For the Little Seven carrier group, CAB-controlled variables were significant, explaining 58 percent of the observed relative profitability, whereas firm-effect variables were significant at the $F.05$ level but not at the $F.01$ level.[3]

The upshot of this important calculation is that the set of actions available to the carriers' managements had relatively little potential to improve their prospects in the airline business. The carriers responded in two ways: they competed strongly along the dimensions they could control, and they angled for favorable regulatory decisions along the other dimensions. This was a far more severe problem for the larger carriers, which had less CAB protection and thus much lower aggregate returns.

In the mid-1960s, there was substantial competition along the dimensions controlled by the carriers. Initially, this took the form of equipment competition, as new jet aircraft and later wide-bodied jet aircraft lowered operating costs and appealed to passengers. Toward the later 1960s, the airlines shifted their competition toward schedule and capacity contests. In the absence of fare competition, the market share of a dominant carrier tended to be more than proportional to the schedule frequency (the S-curve effect). Thus, once the carriers had fully equipped themselves with jet aircraft, they were driven to keep adding aircraft until they were constrained by the inability to finance new equipment or the inability of manufacturers to supply more planes.[4] This dynamic continuously drove down the industry's returns (particularly the large carrier returns), except in the few years in which there was a supply constraint on new equipment.

The second way in which carriers competed was by trying to obtain favorable regulatory decisions. The large carriers tended to prosper if they had several long-haul, near-monopoly routes, while yields were also significant determinants of profitability.[5] Long-haul routes were particularly desirable because, although fares tapered with distance, the operating costs of large, wide-bodied jets tapered even more sharply. Thus, a carrier with a substantial market share on such routes could achieve high load factors and high profits. The most desirable long-distance routes at the time stretched across the Pacific. These were particularly attractive, because Asia was seen as a region of rapidly increasing U.S. trade and involvement, and there was a substantial opportunity for the development of pleasure travel to Hawaii and other destinations. Because the pleasure market generally is more

Table 3-3
Portion of Carrier-Relative Profitability Explained by CAB- and Management-Controlled Variables, 1955–1965

Source of R2	Cumulative R2	Addition to R2 Due to Variables Added	Degrees of Freedom	Mean Square	Computed F	Critical F.05	Critical F.01
Big Four Carriers							
(1) CAB-controlled variables	.84	.84	6	.14000	28.00	2.55	3.76
(2) Management-controlled variables	.87	.03	3	.01000	2.00	3.05	4.82
(3) Firm-effect variables	.89	.02	4	.00500	1.00	2.82	4.31
(4) Unexplained	1.00	.11	22	.00500			
Total	1.00	1.00	35				
Little Seven Carriers							
(5) CAB-controlled variables	.58	.58	6	.09666	16.47	2.30	3.22
(6) Management-controlled variables	.61	.03	3	.01000	1.70	2.81	4.24
(7) Firm-effect variables	.73	.12	7	.01714	2.92	2.22	3.05
(8) Unexplained	1.00	.27	46	.00587			
Total	1.00	1.00	62				
Eleven Domestic Trunk Carriers							
(9) CAB-controlled variables	.56	.56	6	.09333	26.00	2.21	3.04
(10) Management-controlled variables	.60	.04	3	.01333	3.71	2.72	4.04
(11) Firm-effect variables	.72	.12	11	.01091	3.04	1.91	2.48
(12) Unexplained	1.00	.28	78	.00359			
Total	1.00	1.00	98				

Source: William E. Fruhan, Jr., *The Fight for Competitive Advantage*. Boston: Division of Research, Harvard Business School, 1972, Table 2.5 p. 64. Reprinted by permission.

price-sensitive than the business travel market, the airlines expected that large, wide-bodied aircraft with low operating costs would stimulate demand. It was also important that the Pacific Basin air carriers of foreign nations were not so strong or dominant as the European carriers on the North Atlantic.

The Transpacific Route Investigation in the 1960s was a central event in this competition.[6] Traditionally, in its route policies, the CAB attempted to balance the industry by strengthening the weaker carriers. It did this by giving them access to the stronger carriers' better routes. The notion of "historical interest" in an area was related to this. Although this idea originally referred to a route fitting into a carrier's route system, it evolved into a measure of a carrier's ability to develop a route, and the CAB frequently used it as a convenient rationalization for strengthening smaller carriers.[7] Historical interest could be established through having a preexisting feeder system; with the advent of wide-bodied, long-distance jet aircraft, however, almost any system could be argued to feed into almost anywhere. Therefore, the CAB's search for evidence of route development ability focused more on such factors as a carrier's ability to offer low prices, ability to provide accommodations, and knowledge of the local market area. If possession of a fleet of low-cost, wide-bodied jet aircraft was requisite for offering low prices, then travel-related diversification, such as hotel ownership, was seen by the carriers as necessary to convince the CAB that they could develop the market. In addition, some carriers viewed diversification as a way to avoid the "catch-22" posed by the historical interest affinity test: the chief way to gain new routes was to demonstrate a historical interest in an area, and the chief way to establish a historical interest was to serve the area. Several carriers, such as Eastern, saw the siting of hotels in such coveted distant regions such as Hawaii as a way out of this dilemma.[8]

In the original 1961 transpacific award, the CAB had allowed United, Pan American, and Western to serve the U.S. mainland–Hawaii route. A fourth applicant, Hawaiian Airlines, was denied certification because it had no jet equipment. This case was reopened in 1966, because the CAB was disturbed about high fares, high load factors, and high traffic growth. By this time, all carriers had jets, and almost every domestic carrier was a party to the case; a total of eighteen carriers applied for nearly every major Pacific route. Many carriers undertook Type I diversification as part of this effort.

Diversification Pattern

During the mid to late 1960s, all of the large carriers and two of the smaller ones sited hotels and other travel-related facilities as part of their route development efforts. This took two forms: Eastern, American, United, Trans

World, and Continental developed hotels in an effort to secure or protect coveted routes; Braniff and Continental built hotels in an effort to develop traffic on high-potential, long-haul, near-monopoly routes (Continental had a mixed motive).

The Eastern Airlines effort typified the large carriers' moves to develop hotels in an attempt to obtain transpacific routes. Eastern had chronically substandard returns in the period leading up to diversification, stemming from a damaging series of strikes, equipment problems, and, most important, a fundamentally deficient route structure disproportionately composed of congested short-haul routes. The CAB had used Eastern's best routes to nourish the very high performing Delta. Eastern saw in transpacific routes an opportunity to turn this problem around. The importance of the routes to Eastern (as perceived by the carrier's management) and the strategy it intended to build around them were described by Eastern in 1966 as follows:

> Our applications would link the industrial heart of the United States by direct Great Circle routes from New York and the eastern seaboard via Mexico to New Zealand and Australia in the south and, in the north, from Atlanta and the South following a line through Seattle to Japan. These two Great Circle arms would be joined along the western edge of the Pacific by a pattern of service from Japan to Taiwan, Hong Kong, the principal cities of Southeast Asia, including Saigon and Bangkok, and south to Australia. *This great transportation system in the Pacific would have Hawaii as its hub;* Eastern flights from the 50th state would reach to Seattle, Sydney, Tokyo and Manila. We have also applied to link the industrial heart of the United States with Hawaii by direct nonstop jet service from principal cities on the Eastern system.
>
> The most extensive of Eastern's route development efforts are our applications to the Civil Aeronautics Board to provide a wholly new concept of air service for the Pacific. The Pacific Ocean area is the fastest-growing air travel market in the world and is of great and growing economic and strategic significance to our country. As such, it is of increasing importance to the citizens and businesses of the eastern half of the United States, which Eastern serves so comprehensively.
>
> There is a compelling logic to these service proposals. Our country is increasingly committed in the Pacific and particularly in Southeast Asia. Australia is increasingly oriented toward the United States; American investment in the economy of this important Pacific ally now totals more than $1.5 billion. Yet there exists no direct U.S. flag routing from the vital industrial and population heart of the United States to Australia, and no American carrier currently offers a truly comprehensive air service to the Pacific area as a whole.[9] (emphasis added)

To establish its credentials for these important transpacific routes, Eastern took several steps. In 1966, Eastern graduated its first class of stewardesses recruited from Hawaii. It began reequipping with DC-8 aircraft and expressed a willingness to move quickly into long-distance DC-8-62 aircraft that were capable of reaching Hawaii directly from the East Coast, overflying the traditional West Coast gateways.[10]

In 1967, as a final measure, Eastern entered the hotel business, acquiring an 80 percent interest in the Dorado Beach Hotel in Puerto Rico and a 60 percent interest in the Mauna Kea Beach Hotel in Hawaii from Laurance Rockefeller. It also acquired a 40 percent interest in Rockresorts, Inc., the hotel management concern that managed all the Rockefeller resort properties. Charles Simons, former vice-chairman of Eastern Airlines, stated that Eastern went into the hotel business because of the transpacific route case. Along with all other carriers, it interpreted the CAB approach as awarding routes to carriers who had an integrated consumer package. Therefore, hotel ventures became "the fashionable way to go," and, since Eastern had route aspirations in the Pacific, it developed hotel interests in Hawaii. Mr. Simons also noted that before the transpacific case, Pan American was the only carrier with hotel interests; in direct response to the transpacific case, however, American acquired hotel interests in the Pacific area, as did United, Continental, and others.[11]

United's initial entry into the hotel business appears to conform to Mr. Simon's observations on the transpacific route case. Before its purchase of the Western International Hotel chain in 1970, United's pilot hotel development consisted of hotels in Honolulu and San Francisco in 1968. At that time, United's very lucrative Hawaiian routes were threatened by competitive route awards. Thus, this initial development had strong elements of a defensive maneuver in route proceedings. As will be seen, later developments were rooted in causes other than route development.

American pursued a similar strategy in this period. In 1968, at the peak of the transpacific route case, American announced its intention to operate hotels in Acapulco, Seoul, Honolulu, Mexico City, and Long Beach. At that time, American was attempting to gain routes to pleasure destinations. In 1969, the airline stated that it had been "long handicapped in its ability to serve the pleasure traveler."[12]

Trans World Airlines' 1967 acquisition of Hilton Hotels was related to route development in a different area. At that time, Trans World had substantial foreign routes and was actively seeking around-the-world authority in competition with Pan American. Pan American's Intercontinental Hotel chain gave it both competitive and route development advantages. Trans World's acquisition of Hilton's international hotels enabled it to compete on equal footing with Pan American and gave it a parallel ability to develop routes. Although there were multiple reasons for this acquisition, route development and acquisition were important among them.

Continental, a smaller but very active applicant for transpacific routes, pursued a somewhat similar strategy, but with different tactics. Continental tried to get transpacific routes by using Micronesia as a stepping-stone.

In 1967, Continental developed the first international-class hotel in Micronesia. The following year, by its decision in the Pacific Island Local Service Investigation, the CAB gave Continental authority to serve Micronesia. In 1968, Continental announced plans to build six first-class hotels in the Trust Territories. It saw this as a way to generate traffic on its hard-won Micronesian routes, arguing that "travel agents in Japan and the United States see [hotel development] as the key to developing intense traffic."[13]

In a twist, Continental also used this hotel development as an argument for convincing the CAB to grant it further transpacific routes. Continental argued that fostering an eastbound flow of Asian tourists was necessary for full development of Micronesian tourist potential and for filling its hotels. It also pressed for Hawaiian routes at this time. To this end, in 1969, Continental announced its participation with local Hawaiian firms in a joint venture to build a chain of low-priced hotels in Hawaii. This enabled it to match the ability of Eastern, United, and American to offer a full package of services in Hawaii.

Braniff's entry into the hotel business in the late 1960s appears to have been a variation on the route development theme in that it was an attempt to develop business on the routes newly gained when it merged with Panagra. When these routes were first acquired, they were not profitable, as was reflected in Braniff's 1967 return, which was a sharp departure from the trend (see table 3–4). Interview statements by a former senior executive of Braniff indicate that Braniff became convinced that it had to develop traffic on these routes. He argued that Braniff did not develop hotels and restaurants to get routes, because it already had the routes. The problem, as management saw it, was that there was little tourist infrastructure. Thus, the hotel and restaurant business was an addendum to the airline.[14] The former Braniff executive further stated that Braniff's diversification strategy in this period was to provide reasons for people to fly to its destinations.[15] As noted earlier, there was a great incentive to have such long-haul, near-monopoly routes, and battles for them were fierce. Therefore, this development of high-potential routes was consistent with the Type I diversification trend of the time.

In 1967, Eastern was recommended by the CAB examiner for routes between a number of major eastern U.S. points and all points in the South Pacific, including Hawaii. Trans World was recommended for Central Pacific and North Pacific routes; United was given access to Hawaii from several mainland cities; and Western retained its Hawaiian route.[16] The CAB replaced Eastern with American on routes to Japan and eliminated Trans World's North Pacific route. According to Eastern's former vice-chairman, Mr. Simons, the examiner had recommended Eastern for roughly 80 percent of the transpacific routes. Just after that, however, President Johnson took out the CAB chairman to put him in his campaign and replaced him

Table 3–4
Braniff ROE, 1964–1968 (Airline Business Only)

Year	Airline ROE (%)
1964	13.1
1965	17.2
1966	21.4
1967	6.3
1968	12.4

Source: Derived from CAB data.

with a Houston lawyer. When the reconstituted CAB announced the final route awards, Eastern was the only carrier that got nothing. Braniff, a Texas-based carrier, got significant route awards.[17]

The CAB established eight carriers on the mainland–Hawaii route, approving service by all but Eastern, Continental, Delta, and Northeast. Consistent with ongoing policies, the CAB's goal was to strengthen the smaller and weaker carriers; the strong, successful carriers were criticized for lack of initiative and were provided with competition from smaller carriers.[18]

Because international routes were involved, President Johnson had to approve the awards. He disapproved of the addition of a third U.S. flag combination carrier, so the CAB canceled American's authority to Japan. The final set of routes approved by President Johnson had not become effective when President Nixon was inaugurated in 1969, so he undertook to review the decision. Mr. Nixon wanted extensive changes, including having the second carrier route bypass the California gateway. The CAB recommended that Continental serve the routes stretching between Washington, Chicago, Kansas City, Denver, and Phoenix on the one hand, and Hawaii, Samoa, Fiji, New Caledonia, New Zealand, and Australia on the other hand. It reasoned that Continental was aggressively competitive with respect to low-fare policy and the development of tourism.[19] (Continental had developed hotels in Hawaii and Micronesia, and had helped to develop Air Micronesia.)

President Nixon rejected this recommendation and specified that the South Pacific route was to be awarded to a carrier that did not and would not hold California–Hawaii domestic authority (as a result of the transpacific awards). This guideline left the choice between American and Eastern, since the CAB had argued that American's award between California and Hawaii was not necessary and therefore could be eliminated. American was chosen over Eastern because of its financial strength relative to Eastern, its route characteristics, and its potential ability to promote traffic. Ironically, it was argued that American did not possess any significant foreign vacation destinations and therefore could be expected to promote the new route. The decision was approved by President Nixon.[20]

The transpacific route awards led to disastrous consequences for United and Pan American, which had earlier dominated the Hawaiian market. All new carriers assigned their new wide-bodied, long-distance aircraft (chiefly B-747s) to the prime Hawaiian routes. This created a severe overcapacity as competition ratcheted schedule frequencies. In the year of the route awards, Pan American saw its revenues on these routes reduced by $73 million and its operating profits reduced by $25 million.[21] United, which was the dominant carrier on the Hawaiian routes, saw its earnings on these routes plunge from a $19 million profit in 1969 to a $17 million loss in 1970.[22]

The transpacific route decision is important for several reasons. First, it illustrates that the profoundly political nature of the CAB remained intact from earlier days. Second, the Type I diversification it engendered illustrates how fiercely the carriers competed for routes. Finally, it offers background for understanding the later significant diversification undertaken by larger carriers, such as United, which were severely hurt.

Evaluation

Paradoxically, Type I diversification represented a commitment by the air carriers to the airline business. The carriers developed these ventures in an effort to gain routes; thus, they were attempting to "play the regulatory game." Significantly, the big carriers, which were systematically hurt by cross-subsidy, were most active in this movement. The smaller carriers, which systematically benefited from CAB largesse, did not have to bother for the most part. This implies that they saw that the CAB's implicit economic argument—that carriers needed hotels to develop routes—was without substance. Ironically, the CAB itself largely ignored its own route award criteria, and the ultimate decision was basically political.

The carriers' early Type I hotel ventures were largely unprofitable (Hilton International was a key exception). In most cases, they wasted the carriers' resources and distracted their managements' attention from their airline businesses. If any airline managers initially thought they could not get passengers unless they could assure them accommodations, experience provided strong evidence to the contrary. Mr. Simons of Eastern articulated this when he noted that although Eastern carried roughly 40 percent of the air traffic to Puerto Rico, its hotels offered less than 1 percent of the island's hotel rooms. Therefore, he felt that Eastern could "get killed" by the other hotels if it tried to channel traffic to its own hotels. Moreover, he felt that the Dorado Beach was of such high quality that it was usually filled anyway.[23]

Although it could be argued that Braniff's siting of hotels in South America made more economic sense than the CAB's requirement for further development in Hawaii, on balance, regulation-related Type I diversification served little significant social purpose. It did open the door, however, for a much more significant strategic movement of capital out of the industry on the part of the large carriers.

Notes

1. See Fruhan (1972, 62).
2. See Fruhan (1972, p. 64); Northeast was later acquired by Delta.
3. Ibid.
4. See Fruhan (1972, pp. 132–133).
5. See Fruhan (1972, p. 65).
6. See Taneja (1976, pp. 175–180).
7. Ibid.
8. Simons interview (1979).
9. See Eastern Airlines (1966, p. 20).
10. See Eastern Airlines (1967).
11. Simons interview (1979).
12. See American Airlines (1969).
13. See Continental Airlines (1968).
14. Background interview with a senior Braniff executive (1979).
15. Ibid.
16. See Taneja (1976, pp. 175–180).
17. Simons interview (1979).
18. See Taneja (1976, pp. 175–180).
19. Ibid.
20. Ibid.
21. See Pan American Airlines (1970).
22. See United Air Lines (1970).
23. Simons interview (1979).

4
Strategic Groups and Shifting Strategies: Type II Diversification

The period stretching from the 1969 transpacific route awards through the 1976 stirrings of deregulation was a difficult one for the airline industry (see table 4–1). The larger carriers fared much worse than the smaller carriers as problematic regulatory policies continued and as their effects were exacerbated by the 1973 fuel crisis (see table 4–2). This situation was reflected in both the dominant carriers' returns and their market share (as measured by C4). In response to their deteriorating prospects in the airline industry, every one of the large carriers (and Braniff, a small carrier) initiated a fundamental shift in corporate strategy: they allocated resources away from their airline businesses and into nonairline businesses. This resource allocation diversification, or Type II diversification, was very different from the earlier Type I diversification; on balance, it was very beneficial both to the airlines and to society.

Regulation and Intraindustry Competition

The large-carrier strategic group was hurt by the transpacific route awards and by ongoing regulatory problems that eroded the carriers' returns and market share. The transpacific route awards were particularly disastrous for United, Pan American, and Eastern. United and Pan American had previously dominated the routes and had drawn on these returns to cross-subsidize their CAB-mandated marginal routes. Eastern was completely excluded from the route awards and was further hurt when the CAB, in another action, allowed two of Eastern's chief competitors, Delta and Northeast, to merge.

In addition to the specific effects of the transpacific route awards (and Eastern's merger problem), the regulatory problems that had evolved over the years systematically eroded the earnings of the group of dominant carriers and began to alienate them from the industry. The transpacific awards coincided with the industry's massive acquisition of long-haul, wide-bodied jets. Spurred by the S-curve effect, the industry suffered severe overcapacity and excessive competition on many long-haul routes, particularly

Table 4–1
Summary Statistics of All Airlines under Study, 1970–1976

Year	ROE (%)	Growth Rate (%)	C4[a]
1970	0	6	.53
1971	1	(3)	.53
1972	5	25	.53
1973	2	13	.52
1974	5	18	.52
1975	(1)	4	.49
1976	1	14	.49

Source: Derived from CAB data.

[a]C4 = the four-firm concentration ratio, a measure of the proportion of industry revenues captured by the four largest firms.

Table 4–2
Performance Ranking by Strategic Group, 1969–1976

Group	ROE (%)
The Little Six	
Delta	14.8
Braniff	11.3
Northwest	8.2
Western	7.8
National	7.3
Continental	4.2
Mean	8.9
The Big Four	
United	3.5
American	2.7
Trans World	(0.9)
Eastern	(1.1)
Mean	1.1
Other	
Flying Tiger	15.1
Pan American	(6.6)

Source: Derived from CAB data.

the transcontinental and Hawaiian services. Whereas the smaller carriers could fall back on returns earned on CAB-protected routes, the large carriers were increasingly unable to cross-subsidize their thin routes. The CAB's responses only made matters worse, because they did not change the underlying problems.

Faced with the problem of plummeting large-carrier returns (and its attendant publicity), the CAB imposed a de facto moratorium on new competitive route awards. (This effectively ended most Type I diversification.) The CAB also conducted the lengthy Domestic Passenger Fare Investigation, which lasted from 1970 through 1974. In the decision of this investigation, the CAB correctly diagnosed overcapacity as the problem, but its solution was counterproductive. It decided to combat overcapacity by choosing a set of "optimal" load factors and then basing fares on the assumption that these load factors were achieved. Unfortunately, because the CAB left intact the underlying regulatory and structural causes of the large carriers' severe competitive dynamic, this finding did nothing to improve the industry's health.[1]

Confronted with a poorly performing industry, the CAB granted temporary approval for airlines to enter into capacity-limitation agreements on certain routes. American, Trans World, and United were allowed to reduce the number of nonstop flights between New York and Los Angeles, New York and San Francisco, Chicago and San Francisco, and Washington and Los Angeles. In 1972, these agreements were renewed and a similar agreement was undertaken among American, Eastern, and Pan American on the New York–San Juan route. In response to the 1973 fuel shortage that followed the oil embargo, the CAB granted antitrust immunity to the carriers and encouraged them to reduce their schedules. American, Trans World, and United reduced capacity in more than twenty markets.[2]

In July 1975, the CAB refused to extend the capacity agreements, declaring that they were anticompetitive. It cited three reasons for this finding. The first reason was that the level of service had fallen, as evidenced by an increase in multistop flights and by a reduction in the number of off-peak flights instead of peak-hour flights. Second, carriers used the capacity released by agreements to compete more vigorously on routes on which there were no agreements. Third, the CAB was fearful that carriers would take more risks, believing that the CAB would bail them out with capacity agreements.[3]

Ironically, the behavior of the carriers under these agreements was rational and predictable and again reflected the competitive dynamics that regulation had forced on them. It was sensible (from a carrier's perspective) for each carrier to cut off-peak flights and to move capacity onto competitive routes as a protection against the possibility that its competitors would increase their peak schedules. It also was sensible (from a carrier's perspective) not to decrease fares when fuel costs were escalating rapidly and the CAB was lagging in granting compensatory rate increases. To eliminate this sort of behavior and to restore the industry to health, the CAB had to either regulate totally every aspect of the industry or change the rules of the game that determined the intraindustry competitive dynamics. As things stood, the CAB left the dominant carriers increasingly convinced that their long-run prospects in the airline industry were limited.

In addition to the specific regulatory problems of the period, two earlier CAB rate decisions continued to place the dominant carriers at a disadvantage. First, rates had been frozen from 1962 to 1968, and the 1970 onset of the Domestic Passenger Fare Investigation seemed to presage more regulatory lag in rate adjustments. Second, the dominant carriers were hurt by an earlier decision that found strongly in favor of local carriers in splitting joint fares on hauls involving more than one carrier.[4] These ongoing problems reinforced the dominant carriers' beliefs that regulation had permanently turned their airline prospects around and that they must look outside the airline industry for reasonable returns and growth. Interviews with industry executives of this period confirm this link.

Eastern's former vice-chairman, Charles Simons, summed up his view of CAB cross-subsidy by observing that the smaller and weaker carriers of the period had been given the lion's share of the choice new route awards. What sometimes happened, however, was that the smaller carriers could not handle the new routes profitably and so lost more money and thus got even more routes. He cited the example of Northeast, which was awarded some routes for which none of its planes were economically appropriate. At times, it had to fill cargo space with supplementary fuel tanks to fly nonstop on the longer routes. National also got routes that Mr. Simons felt Eastern should have received. In one instance, National was forced to deadhead empty aircraft to the West Coast to position them for eastbound flights, whereas Eastern could have positioned aircraft there in a normal, systematic manner.[5] To make matters worse, Delta, Eastern's rapidly growing competitor, inherited many of these routes when it received CAB permission to merge with Northeast, another major competitor. At that point, Eastern began diversifying.

Rexford Bruno, UAL's former senior vice-president for finance and administration, expressed his firm's perception of the effect of regulation on his firm when he stated that a major reason for United's diversification was that the airline was severely hurt by regulation. In particular, he believed that regulation was stopping United's growth. Because United was the largest airline, the CAB gave it no new routes, giving new routes to the smaller carriers instead. He cited the CAB decision in the transpacific route case as particularly damaging to United, because the CAB let five new competitors into United's very lucrative Hawaiian routes.[6] The CAB also ruled that because of its size, United should not be considered for any new routes to the Far East. United acted to alleviate its regulatory problems: it pushed for deregulation and it diversified.

American similarly saw diversification as an alternative made necessary by limited prospects in the regulated airline industry. Throughout the early 1970s, American developed hotels. In 1976, American's chairman, Albert Casey, was quoted as follows:

> They [the CAB] tell us where to go and how much to charge. We're not going to get any 12% growth like we got in the Sixties for a while. This year [1976] we had 10.4% but from a low base; next year [1977] we're looking for 5.5%.[7]

Restricted prospects in this period had caused American's cash flow to exceed its airline capital spending opportunities.[8] Soon after, American made a substantial nonairline acquisition.

A former senior executive of Braniff explained why the smaller, relatively profitable carrier looked to nonairline diversification, stating that Braniff diversified because it could no longer grow in the airline business. In the early to mid-1970s there were no new route awards. Braniff's management had to decide what to do with its additional capital, people, funds, and resources. It decided that diversification was the best long-term strategy and that Braniff should do more than just fly airplanes.[9]

Between 1964 and 1968, Braniff grew at a compound growth rate of 21.8 percent, the highest in the industry. Expecting continued growth at this pace, Braniff laid on substantial new capacity and resources. When the CAB established a de facto moratorium on competitive route awards in 1970, Braniff's overcapacity led it to its first loss in decades. Also, Braniff's growth rate between 1969 and 1974 was the second lowest in the industry. Although Braniff was profitable, it does not appear to have been able to shift from a high-growth orientation to a profitable, slow-growth strategy, such as Northwest's. Thus, the very dramatic decrease in growth explains Braniff's perception that regulation was restricting its prospects and explains why it continued to diversify despite its relative profitability. Ultimately, this orientation drove Braniff into bankruptcy when it was freed by deregulation.

Confronted with diversifying air carriers, the CAB conducted the Air Carrier Reorganization Investigation in the early 1970s. (This proceeding is analyzed in appendix A.) The CAB's chief concern was that the public interest be served and that air carriers not decrease their service. In the long run, diversification would have allowed carriers to raise their marginal returns on their airline investments to the level obtainable in the rest of the economy. Facing a choice between a healthy industry and extensive service, however, the CAB chose to maximize service, and it imposed a set of rules to govern transactions between air carriers and intracorporate affiliates. These rules were designed to limit diversification and to keep capital in the industry. The issue became moot, however, when the courts overturned the CAB's decision in a lawsuit brought by United.

Diversification Pattern

In response to a perceived lack of airline opportunities, all of the dominant carriers and one small carrier developed Type II diversification in this period. They accomplished this basic shift in corporate strategy in two ways: they either developed diversification de novo or substantially expanded existing Type I diversification in directions that diverged from those of their airline businesses. Table 4–3 provides an overview of the degree of diversification of each strategic group for the years 1972–1976.

Eastern Airlines, which had suffered chronically low returns in its airline business in this period, expanded its hotel holdings by developing the Cerromar Beach Hotel and condominiums in Puerto Rico in 1972. In the

Table 4–3
Airline Revenue as a Percentage of Corporate Revenue, by Strategic Group, 1972–1976

Group	1972	1973	1974	1975	1976
The Little Six					
Delta	100.0	100.0	100.0	100.0	100.0
National	100.0	100.0	100.0	100.0	100.0
Northwest	100.0	100.0	100.0	100.0	100.0
Western	100.0	100.0	100.0	100.0	100.0
Continental	99.2	99.2	99.2	99.2	99.3
Braniff	99.7	99.3	99.4	99.3	99.1
Mean	99.8	99.8	99.8	99.8	99.7
The Big Four					
Eastern	NR[a]	98.2	98.2	NR[a]	100.0
American	90.8	88.3	88.7	88.7	89.3
United	94.4	94.4	93.8	91.0	88.2
Trans World	87.0	77.0	71.0	70.0	70.0
Mean	92.8	89.5	87.9	87.2	86.9
Other					
Flying Tiger	61.9	59.0	54.7	55.2	57.6
Pan American	93.8	93.6	93.2	92.7	91.6

Source: Derived from SEC reports.
[a]NR = not reported; assumed to be 99.0 percent for calculation of mean.

same year, it established a warehousing subsidiary, National Distribution Services, to exploit opportunities in other areas of the transportation business. Both of these ventures remained small, and they were curtailed in 1975 for two reasons: both had been consistently unprofitable because of managerial problems, and the airline itself suffered continuing losses. Eastern's management felt that it did not have the time or resources to establish a major diversifying venture and also keep the airline running.[10]

American, which also experienced a dismal series of earnings in the early 1970s, accelerated its diversification. In 1972, it acquired the four Americana Hotels in Florida, San Juan, and New York. During 1972 and 1973, it developed seven other hotels, and rapid development continued through 1976. Despite its efforts, however, losses mounted in this business. In this period, Sky Chefs reoriented its strategy to conform with American's corporate diversification strategy. It conducted a major effort to expand business with outside customers, and at one point earned about 50 percent of its revenues from other sources. Continuing this trend, American acquired the oil and gas interests of the Republic Corporation in 1976.

United also sharply accelerated its diversification in this period in the face of declining earnings. In 1970, it acquired Western International Hotels, a sizable chain that has since been renamed Westin. Soon thereafter, the hotel chain embarked on a major expansion program, doubling its number of hotel rooms. Western International Hotels remained profitable in this period. In 1975, United purchased GAB Business Services, an insurance adjustment firm.

Trans World, which posted a net loss in this period, steadily diversified as well. Throughout the period, Trans World rapidly expanded its very profitable Hilton International chain, and in 1975, it acquired the Canteen Corporation. This was part of a corporate strategy whose articulated goal was to achieve $100 million in pretax earnings from nonairline consumer business by 1980.[11]

Braniff is a more complex case. It far outperformed the industry in all years except 1970; yet, in this period, Braniff took steps to diversify further. It continued to develop traffic on its long-haul routes to underdeveloped destinations by, as one former executive put it, providing "reasons for people to fly there."[12] By 1974, however, Braniff had developed or acquired hotels in Acapulco, Austin, New Orleans, Orlando, Tucson, and Dallas–Fort Worth. Since these were hardly destinations in need of tourist infrastructure, it is clear that the hotel venture had by then taken on a life of its own in the sense that it no longer merely served the route development and traffic needs of the airline. Braniff also developed Braniff Educational Systems to offer training courses in both airline-related and nonairline-related fields, and started a venture in resort and condominium development.

Braniff's growth orientation explained why it diversified while it was profitable.

In this period, Continental continued its Type I diversification program as it continued to press for international transpacific routes. It completed its hotel-building program in Micronesia and argued that the transpacific routes were necessary to develop the tourist potential of the area and to fill its hotels. (In 1978 and 1979, these efforts came to fruition when Continental was granted authority to serve Asian points through Micronesia; within a few years of the award, Continental sold these Type I hotel holdings.)

The airline industry's diversification pattern largely reflects the systematic profitability differentials created by CAB regulation. During this period, Delta, Northwest, Western, and National—all smaller, profitable carriers—remained single-business airline firms.

Pan American and Tiger International

The experiences of Pan American and Tiger International confirm the basic trends in the trunk airline industry, although they operated in quite different segments of the business. Each firm saw regulation as curtailing its air carrier opportunities, and each diversified substantially as a result.

Pan American is a large U.S.-based international airline that earned poor returns throughout the decade ending in 1976. The chief reasons for this poor record were (1) that the CAB constantly barred it from developing or acquiring a domestic feeder system, (2) that it competed against subsidized carriers of other nations, and (3) that international regulation discouraged innovation. In response, Pan American steadily developed its profitable Intercontinental Hotels chain and performed contract services for other parties. This led to a steady decline in its airline revenue as a proportion of its total revenue during this period.

Paradoxically, Tiger International, an air freight company, was both the most profitable and the most diversified firm under study during the decade ending in 1976. The reasons for this are complex and bear detailed analysis. At the time, the CAB regulated air freight along the lines of passenger airline regulation—controlling routes, rates, and the allowable degree of vertical integration (for example, affiliated trucking).

Initially, the CAB allowed Tiger to provide scheduled service only to a small, unprofitable region consisting of the middle and northern tier of the U.S. domestic market. All of its international business had to be performed on a charter basis with agencies such as the Military Airlift Command (MAC). Rates were also problematic. The CAB standard used to set air cargo rates was the low marginal cost of passenger airlines' belly cargo operations. Tiger, as an all-cargo airline, had to cover higher full costs. With a truncated route structure and inadequate rates, Tiger consistently lost money in its scheduled business. It earned its high overall returns, however, on its military charters, which supported the Indochina war.

When Wayne Hoffman was brought into Tiger as chairman in 1967, he attempted to build Tiger's scheduled commercial business as a hedge against declining U.S. military activities in Southeast Asia. He applied for routes to Honolulu, Guam, Japan, South Korea, Taiwan, Hong Kong, Thailand, South Vietnam, Okinawa, and the Philippines. In 1968, however, as the application inched through the slow regulatory decision process, Tiger's exposure was made clear to the firm. In that year, delays in the delivery of DC-8 jets led to a near-total loss of MAC charters, and Tiger's ROE plunged to a negative 12.6 percent. This led to Tiger's 1968 decision to diversify. Reflecting on this period, Mr. Hoffman observed that Tiger wanted to diversify because many critical airline variables were outside management's control.[13]

Tiger acquired North American Car company in 1970 and aggressively expanded it by both acquisition and internal development. During the early 1970s, it continued to develop its scheduled international routes and to press for new domestic routes in an effort to achieve domestic profitability. Although the international routes were granted, the domestic applications were denied. The CAB's denial of Anchorage routes was particularly frustrating, since this city was already a major hub for Tiger's international operations. Rate regulation problems continued, not only because rates were still based on the relatively low marginal cost of belly cargo, but also because the CAB would not let Tiger rapidly pass on fuel cost increases to its very price-insensitive but service-sensitive customers. (In consequence, it had to reduce service.) Tiger saw its earnings plunge from an ROE of over 20 percent during the period from 1971 through 1973 to far less than half that in the succeeding three years. Consequently, in 1976, Tiger diversified further, purchasing the Investor's Mortgage Insurance Company.

Evaluation

The period from 1969 to 1976 was one of slow growth and fierce competition for the larger carriers but one of profitability for the smaller carriers, as the latter group reaped the benefits of protected routes and competitive route awards. Consistent with the strategic framework presented in chapter 1, all of the Big Four carriers initiated or continued substantial diversification in the face of sharply subaverage profitability and growth. The large carriers perceived that the CAB had condemned them to low returns through competitive route awards and had put a cap on their growth, and the statistical record shows that this was a realistic view. Faced with a zero-sum game competition that they were losing, they diversified to raise returns and to continue growth. Meanwhile, most of the smaller carriers— Delta, Northwest, National, and Western—exhibited strong profitability. As expected, none of these smaller carriers diversified at all.

The Type II diversification undertaken by the dominant carrier strategic group was beneficial both to the carriers and to society. It enabled resources to flow into industries in which they could be employed more productively and thus could earn higher rates of return (see chapter 8). Where sound investments were made (see chapter 7), the carriers earned higher overall returns, and society gained a more efficient allocation of resources. Poorly performing investments, such as Eastern's, represented implementation problems rather than flaws in the underlying corporate strategies.

Continental and Braniff, the other smaller carriers, were relatively profitable but remained diversified. Continental continued to pursue a Type I diversification strategy to develop traffic on its hard-won Micronesian routes. Also, as a clear loser in the transpacific route case, it continued to press (with eventual success) for Asian routes, arguing that these were necessary for full development of its Micronesian destinations. Braniff, though profitable in this period, saw its growth rate nosedive from 21 percent to 5 percent as it was rapidly laying on capacity to cover expected growth. This caused profitability problems and convinced Braniff that it had to look elsewhere for coveted growth.

Continental's continued Type I diversification is not problematic, but, rather, anachronistic. It represented a commitment to the airline industry itself, as did other carriers' earlier Type I diversification. Braniff, however, is more anomalous. By diversifying for short-term growth rather than for long-term returns, Braniff chose to lower its overall profitability. (This assumes that as a favored smaller carrier, its prospective long-run airline returns were higher than those available elsewhere, which turned out to be the case.) This was a strategic error for Braniff; the firm seems to have made a long-run strategic decision in response to a short-term problem. As it turned out, the strategy was not well implemented either. Neither Braniff nor society benefited from Braniff's Type II diversification.

Pan American and Tiger both faced difficult and uncertain prospects in their air carrier businesses as a result of regulation, although Tiger's charter business gave it a good measure of profitability. Pan American's diversification raised its returns, which benefited both society and the airline. Tiger's diversification raised its returns and hedged it against uncertainties in the air freight business. Although Tiger was hurt by marginal cost pricing of air cargo, the CAB's marginal price was best for society if substantial low-marginal-cost capacity was available from passenger airplanes' belly space. In this instance, diversification was a realistic and proper response for both society and Tiger.

In all, a strong, well-implemented program of diversification had the potential to raise the dominant carriers' returns up to those available in other industries and to reduce airline industry overcapacity.[14] (The observed program represented deliberate movement in this direction.) In this way, the level of service offered would have equilibrated with the level economically demanded. This would have put continuing pressure on smaller carriers to run efficient operations, rather than looking to cross-subsidy to ensure returns. (Northwest and Delta have always run efficient operations.) Structuring themselves in a tight, efficient manner would have led to a more productive use of resources for society and would have positioned the smaller carriers to compete in a deregulated industry. Thus, Type II diversification would have benefited all concerned.

Notes

1. See Taneja (1976, pp. 189–216).
2. Ibid., pp. 57–59.
3. Ibid.
4. See Johnson (1974, ch. 13).
5. Simons interview (1979).
6. Bruno interview (1979).
7. *Forbes*, 11/15/76.
8. See American Airlines (1976).
9. Background interview with a senior Braniff executive (1979).
10. Simons interview (1979).
11. Trans World Corporation (1979).
12. Braniff executive interview (1979).
13. Hoffman interview (1979).
14. See Fruhan (1972).

5
Deregulation

D eregulation had a profound effect on the airlines. As administrative actions and legislation methodically removed regulation's artificial influences on the industry's key competitive forces, the various airlines' prospects within the industry shifted greatly. Almost every carrier had to alter its intraindustry competitive strategy fundamentally so that it rested on new and defensible competitive strengths that were appropriate for the new environment. To make the transition to the new set of airline competitive strategies, many carriers also had to alter their corporate diversification strategies. A carrier that increased its airline presence to develop wider opportunities in the airline industry could draw resources from its diversification, while a carrier that focused on lucrative smaller airline industry niches could shift its excess airline resources into increased diversification. In this manner, a company could adjust its interindustry corporate strategy to reflect a new equilibrium in opportunities.

In practice, however, several firms had trouble managing the transition into deregulation (table 5–1). These companies' problems stemmed from difficulties in recasting their intraindustry competitive strategies and in adjusting their corporate diversification strategies to ease the transition. The adjustment difficulties were exacerbated by a series of severe external problems that buffeted the industry during the 1979–1982 transitional period, leaving little margin for strategic error (table 5–2). Substantial fuel price increases, the DC-10 grounding, the PATCO (air traffic controllers) traffic restrictions, a weak economy, and high interest rates all hurt the industry greatly.[1] By 1984, the industry was emerging from its transitional period with a new set of corporate and competitive strategies.

This chapter analyzes the effect of deregulation on the airline industry, illustrating the use of the strategic framework in both a deregulated and a regulated context. First, we will analyze the changes that deregulation brought to the airline industry and use the strategic framework to generate normative prescriptions for the firms in the industry. Then, we will evaluate the successes and failures of the industry in light of the framework's suggestions. The analysis is presented in detail because it is very relevant

Table 5–1
Performance Ranking by Strategic Group, 1977–1983

1977–1979		1980–1983	
Group	*ROE (%)*	*Group*	*ROE (%)*
The Little Six		*The Little Six*	
Western	18.8	Delta	4.7
Delta	15.6	Northwest	2.8
Continental	9.4	Western	(36.0)
Northwest	8.7	Braniff	Bankrupt
Braniff	7.4	Continental	Bankrupt
National	4.7	National	Merged
Mean	10.8	Mean	NM[a]
The Big Four		*The Big Four*	
Eastern	12.1	American	2.6
American	11.3	United	(1.6)
United	9.9	Trans World	(6.4)[b]
Trans World	7.6	Eastern	(21.9)
Mean	10.2	Mean	(6.8)
Other		*Other*	
Flying Tiger	12.4	Flying Tiger	(36.7)
Pan American	10.4	Pan American	(39.2)

Source: Derived from CAB and SEC data. Adjustments have been made to make the figures comparable, which may cause some to differ somewhat from reported amounts.
[a]NM = not meaningful
[b]By 1983 Delta was larger than Trans World

Table 5–2
Summary Statistics of All Airlines under Study, 1977–1983

Year	*ROE (%)*	*Growth Rate (%)*	*C4*[a]
1977	11	14	.49
1978	18	14	.49
1979	4	12	.45
1980	(1)	19	.46
1981	(6)	5	.44
1982	(17)	(2)	.44
1983	(5)	7	.46

Source: Derived from CAB data.
[a]C4 = the four-firm concentration ratio, a measure of the proportion of industry revenues captured by the four largest firms.

to several other industries that are in the process of deregulation (see chapter 8).

Deregulation and Airline Industry Structure

Under the leadership of John Robson, the CAB took the first steps toward deregulation in 1976, when it began loosening controls (particularly fare restrictions) on the airlines. These early actions were followed up strongly by the next CAB chairman, Alfred Kahn. Meanwhile, Senator Kennedy, Senator Cannon, and Representative Anderson spearheaded a drive to deregulate the industry and to abolish the CAB. These efforts led to passage of the Airline Deregulation Act of 1978 (Public Law No. 95-504), which pushed off the industry on a five-year voyage toward complete deregulation.

Several factors combined in the late 1970s to create an opportunity for deregulation to take place. There was a widespread movement to reform government institutions, which was manifested in efforts to deregulate several industries. In the airline industry, certain key carriers had been advocating deregulation to free themselves from perceived CAB constraints on growth and profits. Rexford Bruno, former senior vice-president of UAL expressed this attitude when he stated that the transpacific route awards and the CAB's de facto moratorium on new route awards led his airline to push for deregulation.[2] Ironically, other important carriers, such as American, argued against deregulation, fearing that they were so weakened by ongoing regulation that they could not survive without the CAB's "safety net."[3] In 1978, a period of unprecedented airline industry prosperity—caused by favorable general economic conditions—convinced many carriers that they could prosper on their own. This, combined with the CAB's loss of an important constituent group of carriers, provided a window for airline industry deregulation.

The changes brought by deregulation significantly affected the airline industry's economic structure and the prospects of the individual carriers. Deregulation altered the forces that determined the performance of the airlines, and this forced the carriers to adjust their intraindustry competitive strategies so that they rested on new competitive strengths. Under regulation, the CAB had tightly controlled new entry into the overall industry and into particular city-pair markets. This enabled it to provide the smaller carriers with relatively high, competition-free returns and to cross-subsidize marginal services. Deregulation provided for a three-year transition period during which the carriers could select one new route annually without CAB approval. In the same period, each carrier could designate one of its existing routes to be closed to new competition. Carriers also could acquire dormant route authorities of other airlines.[4] These measures led to a lifting of government-created barriers to entry, exposing the overall industry to new competitors from outside the industry and exposing individual carriers to increased competition in particular markets.

The removal of regulatory barriers to entry forced the airlines to take steps to construct new entry barriers that were capable of protecting their competitive positions and insulating them against destructive direct price competition. There were several areas in which the deregulated carriers were exposed and several potential barriers that they could develop. High-density, point-to-point routes (particularly long-haul routes) were most exposed to new entry.[5] Hub-and-spoke feeder systems, on the other hand, afforded a degree of protection resting on both operational (cost) and marketing advantages. Consolidation of sparsely traveled feeder routes (spokes) enabled the dominant airline at a hub to achieve higher load factors on the line-hauls.[6] The dominant carrier also could achieve fuller utilization of terminal services, although, ironically, this advantage was lessened by the practice of selling terminal services to other carriers. The complex and costly interchange and reservation systems required in a feeder system provided both absolute capital barriers against new entrants and the ability to implement sophisticated, flexible price discrimination schemes based on the demand patterns for individual flights.[7] Again, ironically, the practice of selling reservation system participation tended to lessen the latter advantage. In addition, the intensive local marketing necessary in a hub-and-spoke operation led to some marketing economies of scale and to "market presence," whereby individual carriers were identified with their hub markets. This was partially based on the *S*-curve effect, in which a dominant airline's market share was more than proportional to its capacity.

Carriers that offered wide service through comprehensive and ubiquitous networks potentially could erect product differentiation entry barriers by developing a perceived service advantage.[8] (Frequent flier programs could further tie travelers to wide-service carriers.) In practice, however, carriers that sought to base their strategies on wide-service advantages during the transitional deregulation period achieved success only when their route systems rested on multiple strong hubs. This might seem to imply that the geographically focused market presence advantage inherent in a local hub operation was really the crucial factor and that successful wide-service carriers merely linked hubs. It is more likely, however, that the large, established carriers' relatively high costs of operations in the early deregulation period made it difficult for them to compete on linear routes against low-cost, nonunion carriers and established carriers that had excess capacity. As the differential between the costs of existing and new carriers erodes, and as capacity equilibrates, wide service will likely provide an increasing advantage beyond that which results from linking strong hubs. (The reversal of the trend in the C4 measure in table 5–2 suggests this possibility.)

Airlines could also differentiate themselves by appealing to particular segments of the travel market with advertising, pricing, and services tailored to meet their particular needs. Airlines seeking business travelers could offer high-priced but highly available service (such as the Eastern Shuttle), while those seeking vacation travelers could offer lower-priced services with lower service standards (less frequency or fewer amenities).[9]

Sophisticated travel agent reservation systems provided another potential barrier to entry. Besides enabling carriers to construct flexible price discrimination programs for individual flights, these systems enabled them to dominate the channels of distribution for their products. The systems' programs were carefully designed to display, first, the offerings of the carrier that provided the system, increasing the likelihood of a booking. (In 1983, under pressure from the CAB, American and others agreed to remove this bias from their systems.[10])

It is important to note that the airline industry is not characterized by great economies of scale, with the limited exceptions of terminal operations (which can be purchased from other carriers) and marketing. This implies that airlines cannot achieve insurmountable long-run cost advantages from large size alone.

Buyer bargaining power shifted dramatically with deregulation. Through their representatives in Congress, numerous marginal buyers (infrequent passengers from outlying regions) had pressured the CAB into providing inexpensive service on relatively sparse routes. This service was cross-subsidized by relatively price-insensitive customers on denser routes. Deregulation generally allowed a carrier to stop serving a city after giving a ninety-day notice,[11] and commuter airlines were made eligible for subsidies for serving unprofitable markets.[12] When deregulation lifted the barriers to exit from marginal markets, the barriers to entry into prime markets, and fare restrictions, buyer power shifted from a political basis to an economic one. New entrants and established carriers entered prime, high-density, linear routes and competed fares down, while the established carriers withdrew from their marginal routes. Through this dynamic, economically strong buyers gained more value in their air transportation purchases, while economically weak buyers saw service fall to economically supportable levels. The emergence of focused, differentiated carriers with targeted offerings meant even more value for strong buyers, such as frequent business travelers. Frequent-flier programs also increased the value received by this particularly desirable segment.[13] Currently, major corporations are starting to contract for capacity on very favorable terms, much as major tour operators have done traditionally.[14] This transformation of buyer bargaining power signaled the end of cross-subsidy as a viable policy.

Deregulation altered supplier bargaining power, although labor's substantial entrenched power slowed the adjustment. Federal compensatory payments of up to six years' duration were provided in cases where deregulation reduced an airline's work force by as much as 7.5 percent.[15] Under regulation, unions had exercised substantial bargaining power based on their political strength, which exceeded their intrinsic economic bargaining power. The CAB, in response, had permitted large wage settlements to be passed on to price-insensitive buyers.

The relatively slow pace of established carrier labor cost adjustment gave the new entrants an important temporary competitive cost advantage (which is quite different from the long-run cost advantage accruing from economies of scale).[16] However, this substantial operational edge (25 percent or more) enabled the new carriers to lower fares and to attract traffic to the point where they have severely depleted the resources of several established carriers and handicapped their ability to move into defensible competitive postures.

Equipment manufacturers also saw deregulation change their bargaining positions. Because the regulated airlines had competed primarily with service rather than with cost, chronic airline overcapacity and overrapid rates of aircraft technological development resulted.[17] Deregulation increased the number of airline buyers and placed pressure on the airlines to obtain lower-cost aircraft. This will likely lead to longer production runs of more standardized aircraft and to the development of new models targeted for particular market niches. At the same time, the market for lower-cost, used, and relatively fuel-efficient (especially in periods of high fuel prices) aircraft will likely rise as cost-oriented carriers scramble for an edge.[18] The net effect will likely be to improve the bargaining power of large, wide-service carriers that can assure economic production runs of new-generation aircraft and can sell their aircraft on an active second-hand market. American's recent very favorable purchase of MD-80 aircraft provides an example of this.[19]

In addition to the long-run changes in supplier relationships, two short-run problems temporarily increased the demand for aircraft during the transitional deregulation period. The established carriers' overall movement away from long and medium-length linear routes and toward hubs necessitated a shift toward short-haul aircraft. This left many carriers with excess long-haul equipment and led to fare wars on overcapacity long-haul routes.[20] By unfortunate coincidence, fuel prices rose dramatically during the transitional deregulation period, making large proportions of several established carriers' fleets obsolete (table 5–3).[21] These problems forced several carriers to decide whether to undertake major reequipment programs or to diminish their presence in the airline industry. Those that chose the former option greatly increased their financial overhead, thus increasing their exposure in the economic downturn that followed.

Interfirm rivalry within the industry was substantially transformed by deregulation. Regulatory cross-subsidy, which largely defined interfirm rivalry in the regulated years, has all but disappeared in deregulation. The

Table 5–3
Proportion of Fuel-Inefficient Jet Capacity, 1979

Airline	Fuel-Inefficient Capacity (%)
Trans World	48.8
American	40.7
Pan American	30.5
Eastern	22.7
United	22.4
Braniff	19.9
National	18.5
Western	15.8
Continental	14.8
Northwest	10.3
Delta	4.5

Source: Meyer and Oster (1981, p. 182). Reprinted by permission.

airlines were given increasing freedom over fares during the transition, which dramatically changed the industry's competitive dynamics. The deregulation act gave the carriers, until fare regulation was scheduled to be phased out at the end of 1982, the freedom to raise fares by as much as 5 percent and to lower them by as much as 50 percent without CAB approval. In markets served by four or more carriers, the carriers were allowed to raise fares by 10 percent.[22] With rapid fuel price increases prevalent in 1979–1980, the base fare level was adjusted through a series of interim policies that reflected increases in both route distance and fuel costs. The effect of fare deregulation was to shift competition from service and capacity to price, and yields plunged relative to costs.[23] At the same time, regulatory lag hindered the carriers' ability to pass along cost increases where feasible. Only in 1983, when industry growth and a measure of prosperity returned, did the carriers move to shift competition away from price. American led this movement by introducing a system of mileage-based fares, which provided a basis for consensus pricing.

The basic shifts in industry structure brought about by deregulation greatly changed the relative positions and prospects of the firms within the industry. Under regulation, cross-subsidy had created two strategic groups. The smaller carriers, which were the recipients of cross-subsidy, had prospered relative to the larger carriers. Deregulation substantially altered the relative advantages of the firms within the two groups but did not systematically reverse them. There were two reasons for this: some of the larger carriers were so depleted of resources that they could not build viable wide-market strategies; and some of the smaller carriers had wisely built sound, defensible, hub-based route structures, had carried conservative capital structures, and had kept costs down. A carrier's prospects in the industry were ultimately determined by its ability to build a defensible competitive strategy, and not merely by the strategic group to which it belonged under regulation. There were both well-positioned and poorly positioned firms in both groups.

The basic competitive strategies available to the carriers were variants of the generic strategies commonly used in competitive industries.[24] These strategies can be sorted along two dimensions: cost versus service, and wide-market versus segment focus. Each strategy has the potential to offer certain competitive advantages that provide barriers preventing others from competing directly, thus enabling a firm to earn higher, protected returns. An individual firm's intraindustry strategic choice depends on the resources and position it carries forward from the earlier (regulated) period, its values, and other firms' strategic positioning relative to the new opportunities and dangers in the industry.

Two wide-market strategies were theoretically available to the airlines. A carrier could attempt to dominate the market with a cost-leadership strategy, in which low costs would enable it either to underprice the market or to make very high profits at prevailing prices (that is, prices that allow costlier carriers to earn only marginal returns). This strategy works best in industries in which there are substantial economies of scale. In such industries, a firm with market share dominance can attain lower costs than other firms that have smaller shares; those low costs, in turn, enable the firm to underprice its competitors, thus gaining even more market share and even lower costs. This strategy is somewhat problematic in the airline industry, because only minor economies of scale are achievable—and even these are canceled somewhat by the common practice of selling terminal and reservation services. Thus, a carrier that is pursuing a cost-leadership strategy must base its competitive advantage on tight cost controls and other management measures. Because cost-controlling managers are frequently hired away by competitors, cost leadership would seem to provide a not insurmountable advantage in the long run. Already, a new generation of labor contracts—such as American's, which provides for hiring new workers at a fraction of the prevailing pay scales—promise to lower the established carriers' costs steadily.

Product differentiation through wide-market, high-quality service is the other basic wide-market competitive strategy available to the airlines. This strategy would seem to offer significant long-term entry barriers, but in practice (as noted earlier), only carriers with wide service based on strong multiple hubs have prospered. When the large, established carriers lower their costs to levels approaching those of the low-cost carriers, and when capacity equilibrates, wide service will likely provide a more decisive advantage. The rather limited size of the market probably implies, however, that no more than three or possibly four carriers can pursue this strategy successfully.

Two focused strategies parallel the two wide-market strategies on a smaller scale. A focused low-cost strategy offers the potential for a carrier to specialize in particular limited services (chiefly high-density, linear routes), attracting large numbers of price-sensitive passengers with low fares. Most new carriers have entered with this strategy. Because these cost advantages are easily copied by other new entrants, however, and because the established carriers can erode many of the new carriers' cost advantages in the long run, this strategy does not promise high long-run returns.

The focused differentiation competitive strategies seem to offer the best prospects for gaining protective entry and mobility barriers and, con= sequently, high long-run returns. The market for passenger air transportation can be segmented along several dimensions. Carriers can focus on geographic segments through hub-and-spoke operations or through international gateway feeder systems. (This substrategy is facilitated when competitors are restricted by scarce gate space.) Alternatively, carriers can segment the market by focusing on price-insensitive but service-sensitive business passengers. Geographic and service segmentation can be combined to focus a carrier's strategy sharply. These focused strategies lead to substantial and enduring operational and marketing advantages that, once in place, are not easily copied by competitors. Thus, they offer the possibility of high long-run returns for a relatively large number of carriers.

Most carriers had to make fundamental changes in their competitive strategies to adapt to deregulation. Two transitional strategies were particularly hazardous. First, continuing to operate with a strategy appropriate for regulation could lead to problems. An airline that maintained a large proportion of high-density, linear routes would be exposed to severe competition, while a carrier that attempted to extend its route system rapidly would be exposed to an increased risk of insolvency. The former strategy implicitly assumed continuing regulatory entry barriers, and the latter strategy implicitly assumed continuing regulatory cross-subsidy as a safety net. A second problematic transitional strategy was mixing competitive strategies, thus operating without a clear direction and trying to be everything to everyone. Multiple strategies tend to cancel each other out and leave the organization without common direction. Companies in this position—"stuck in the middle—" tend to oscillate back and forth between strategies without developing a solid, defensible position.[25] These firms generally earn chronically subnormal returns.

The established airlines' transition to deregulation was made slower and more difficult by several temporary problems, mentioned earlier. First, most established carriers had entrenched labor unions with high pay scales, high seniority, and restrictive work rules. This seriously inhibited their ability to compete in high-density, linear routes against new entrants with substantially lower operating costs. Only massive losses and near bankruptcy induced most carriers' unions to grant substantial concessions in return for significant amounts of equity and representation on the carriers' boards of directors. Continental was forced to declare bankruptcy to cancel its union contracts and to lower its costs. Although this labor cost differential is temporary and eroding, several low-cost new entrants (for example, People Express and New York Air) have gained substantial market positions, while several established carriers (for example, Eastern, Trans World, and Western) have been depleted of resources to the point where they might not be able to implement viable strategies.

Availability of appropriate equipment was a second transitional problem encountered by established carriers.[26] Several established carriers were caught with fleets that were significantly composed of inappropriate long-haul equipment, whereas the new entrants could match their equipment acquisitions to their emerging needs. Moreover, the great fuel cost increases of the period rendered many older aircraft obsolete. (Trans World, American, and Pan American were particularly vulnerable).[27] Both of these factors placed a costly reequipment burden on established carriers, slowing their transition to defensible hub systems, draining resources, and greatly increasing competition (thus lowering yields) on long-haul linear routes.

Two other factors also slowed several established carriers' ability to respond to deregulation. Several carriers' top management teams were unable to formulate new, viable, defensible competitive strategies.[28] Importantly, old-line carrier managements tended to be oriented toward growth rather than profits and frequently sought to extend their route networks rapidly, rather than moving toward profitable niches centered on the strong segments of their businesses. Shortage of gate space in key terminals also inhibited the pace at which certain carriers could adjust their route structures.[29]

As deregulation altered the various carriers' airline prospects, their corporate diversification strategies were required to change as well. Large carriers that were driving toward wide-market competitive strategies could reduce their diversification to the extent to which resources were needed to strengthen and fuel the growth of their airline businesses. Large carriers that were carving out niche strategies could channel excess resources into diversification. Smaller carriers that were building toward market leadership or enlarging protected niches could draw upon their diversification for needed resources, while other smaller carriers that were moving into smaller niches (or finding it more profitable to exit the airline industry entirely) could diversify with resources surplus to their airline needs. Through these actions, the carriers could coordinate their intraindustry competitive strategies and their interindustry corporate strategies to maintain profitability. In practice, however, many carriers merely jerry-rigged their intraindustry competitive strategies to fit the airline resources they carried forward into deregulation, rather than developing sound airline competitive strategies and adjusting their corporate diversification strategies to reflect their new prospects.

Airline Response to Deregulation

The airlines have had very mixed results in their transition into deregulation: almost half of the carriers have been largely successful, and the remainder have had severe and continuing difficulties (see tables 5–1, 5–4, and 5–5). All in all, American, United, Delta, and Northwest, have been successful, while Eastern, Pan American, Braniff, Continental, Western, and Tiger have had serious problems. Trans World, a complex case, falls between the two groups. The reasons for the various carriers' success or failure can be traced directly to the degree to which they moved toward the sound intraindustry airline competitive strategies and interindustry corporate diversification strategies developed here.[30]

Table 5–4
Performance Ranking by Strategic Group, 1983

Group	ROE (%)
The Little Six	
Northwest	8.5
Delta	(1.5)[a]
Western	(66.9)
Braniff	Bankrupt
Continental	Bankrupt
National	Merged
The Big Four	
American	16.2
United	10.7
Trans World	(1.7)[a]
Eastern	(58.0)
Other	
Flying Tiger	(91.0)
Pan American	(16.6)

Source: Derived from CAB and SEC data. Adjustments have been made to make the figures comparable, which may cause some to differ somewhat from reported amounts.
[a]Delta was larger than Trans World in 1983.

Table 5–5
Growth Rate by Strategic Group, 1979–1983

Group	Growth Rate (%)
The Little Six	
Northwest	14.3
Delta	10.0
Western	5.2
Braniff	Bankrupt
Continental	Bankrupt[a]
National	Merged
The Big Four	
United	13.2
American	8.6
Eastern	8.2
Trans World	3.6
Other	
Flying Tiger	22.1
Pan American	8.2

Source: Derived from CAB and SEC data.
[a]Continental's growth rate during 1979–1982 was 7.9 percent.

American and United were large carriers that developed wide-market, quality-service differentiation strategies, drawing upon their corporate diversification (as needed) for resources. Both of these carriers entered deregulation with relatively costly operations and large amounts of debt (American also had a very fuel-inefficient fleet), and both ultimately achieved success under deregulation by developing strong, multiple-hub route systems (see table 5–6).

American moved early in deregulation to build a strong, defensible, hub-based route system. In 1980, the carrier articulated its reasoning for this strategy:

> Long-haul nonstop markets such as American's transcontinental and semi-transcontinental routes are regarded as attractive new business opportunities by established airlines with excess wide-body capacity. . . . Such large point-to-point markets, and some short-haul markets as well, are also attractive to new entrants that are not full service airlines. . . . In effect a connecting center [hub] allows its operator to offer a unique product, one beyond the reach of an airline that specializes in point-to-point nonstop service.[31]

American's early deregulation route strategy centered on building hubs in Dallas/Fort Worth, Chicago, and St. Louis (St. Louis was later dropped).[32] In 1984, American announced plans to develop a third major hub in Denver,

Table 5–6
Financial Leverage, Operating Efficiency, and Current Ratio, 1977

Group	Debt-to-Total-Assets Ratio	Operating Ratio	Current Ratio
The Little Six			
Braniff	.66	8.5	1.20
Continental	.73	6.8	.72
Delta	.58	9.3	.79
National	.17	2.6	1.14
Northwest	.39	10.0	1.44
Western	.67	3.2	1.03
The Big Four			
American	.66	2.7	1.46
Eastern	.69	3.7	.84
Trans World	.71	1.8	1.09
United	.69	2.7	1.50
Other			
Flying Tiger	.80	7.2	1.44
Pan American	.43	4.6	1.19

Source: Debt-to-total assets ratios and current ratios derived from *Moody's Transportation Manual* (1978); operating ratios derived from CAB data.

stating that this was "entirely consistent with our long-term plan of developing a national airline network."[33] To bring its management team close to the epicenter of its new operations, American moved its corporate headquarters from New York to Dallas/Fort Worth.

American took the lead in building a marketing strategy appropriate for its wide-market, product-differentiation competitive strategy. To dominate its channels of distribution, American rapidly developed one of the most popular travel agent reservation systems in the industry, even acquiring, in 1983, a travel agency data-processing system company to make its offering more attractive.[34] In 1983, American introduced a mileage-based pricing system to shift competition toward service and distribution and away from price. American also moved to protect its cost flank by negotiating a labor contract that promised to lower its labor costs to levels comparable with those of many new entrants and by acquiring, on very favorable terms, a very fuel-efficient fleet of MD-80 aircraft.[35] These actions promised that, over the long run, American would be able to hold its own on cost, so that the edge that it gained through wide-service product differentiation would prove decisive.

To support its growing market-leadership airline strategy, American shifted its resources away from its diversification program (table 5–7). In 1979, Albert Casey, American's chairman, stated that he divested the money-losing Americana Hotel chain and refocused Sky Chefs away from

Table 5–7
Airline Revenue as a Percentage of Corporate Revenue, by Strategic Group, 1977–1983

Group	1977	1978	1979	1980	1981	1982	1983
The Little Six							
Delta	100.0	100.0	100.0	100.0	100.0	100.0	100.0
Northwest	100.0	100.0	100.0	100.0	100.0	100.0	100.0
Western	100.0	100.0	100.0	100.0	100.0	100.0	100.0
Braniff	99.1	99.3	99.3	99.9	99.3	BKT	BKT
Continental	NR	NR	NR	NR	NR	NR	BKT
National	100.0	100.0	100.0	Merged	Merged	Merged	Merged
Mean	99.8	99.8	99.8	99.9	99.8	99.9	100.0
The Big Four							
Eastern	100.0	100.0	100.0	100.0	100.0	100.0	100.0
American[a]	89.7	90.1	94.1	96.2	95.5	95.2	95.2
United	88.5	88.0	86.0	88.4	88.3	88.3	89.2
Trans World	70.0	68.7	68.4	67.2	66.7	65.0	64.0[b]
Mean	87.1	86.7	87.1	88.0	87.6	87.1	87.1
Other							
Flying Tiger	55.8	58.0	50.9	45.6	55.3	59.5	70.4
Pan American	86.8	86.6	85.5	88.4	92.5	91.4	91.0

Source: Derived from CAB and SEC data.

Note: BKT = bankrupt. NR = not reported; assumed to be 99.5 percent for calculation of mean.

[a]Includes intracompany sales of Sky Chefs to American Airlines.

[b]Theoretical calculation; TWA was spun off as an independent company, but Trans World Corporation retained links in 1983.

its other customers to pursue the opportunities that deregulation offered the airline:

> American Airlines is committed to the airline. . . . The airline absorbs all of [American's] efforts because of noise regulations and deregulation. . . . American is committed to the airline because that business requires a critical mass which it has already committed, and it is hard to get out of the business.[36]

At the time, he observed that the operating ratio is the key figure in the airline business. He noted that because Northwest, Braniff, and Delta were achieving operating returns of 8 to 9 percent while American achieved only 4 percent, American was very exposed and required all of its resources to build its market position in the airline industry. He kept American's oil and gas business, however, because it was relatively risk-free (it was purchased with a nonrecourse note) and because he felt that its trading operations gave the airline an inside track on fuel procurement.[37]

United's early deregulation strategy was problematic, but after a mid-course correction, the airline emerged from the transition period with a successful wide-market, quality-service competitive strategy resting upon multiple strong hubs (similar to American's). Initially, United drove toward a route structure that would have been ideal under regulation but was problematic in a competitive airline industry: it increased its long-haul routes and dropped many of its smaller short-haul feeder markets. In support of this move, it made plans to sell its short-haul B-737 airplanes and to move into longer-range aircraft. However, it retained large connecting hubs in Chicago and Denver and smaller hubs in Memphis, Pittsburgh, and Kansas City (the Kansas City hub was developed in 1978).

By 1981, United faced mounting losses and saw new competition move into its exposed long-haul routes. In response, United started the high-density, low-cost, point-to-point Friendship Express service. At this stage, United was pursuing several strategies at once, attempting to position itself as both a low-cost and a high-service carrier. The airline was very specific in its intent:

> Now United can be many airlines. We have too many competitors to be just one kind of airline. United is being more responsive to the demands of the markets—selling low priced product on some segments (a quality product designed for low price) and a premier product on other segments.[38]

By 1983, faced with continuing poor performance, United shifted strongly toward a multiple-hub feeder route system. It focused its route development efforts on strengthening its primary Chicago, Denver, and San

Francisco hubs by adding spokes, increasing frequency, and adding one-stop flights. The carrier's marketing efforts largely paralleled those of American. It developed a ubiquitous travel agency computer reservations system and strengthened its frequent-traveler program. Those provisions, along with overall economic prosperity, returned United to profitability in 1983.

As UAL focused on repositioning United, it slowed its diversification so that the airline's proportionate share of the corporation's revenues began increasing. Rexford Bruno, former senior vice-president of UAL, stated that deregulation had caused UAL to change its diversification strategy: it stopped searching for acquisitions because it saw many opportunities in the airline business as well as in its hotel and insurance businesses.[39] However, UAL did not divest its nonairline businesses, for several reasons: United was so large that its management was concerned that antitrust or diseconomies of scale might curtail growth; the company had enough capital to reposition the airline without having to sell other subsididaries; the corporation's top managers (Edward Carlson and Richard Ferris) had come from the hotel business and were loyal to it; and the hotel chain was generating substantial returns.[40] Thus, UAL was able to remain diversified while fully developing its airline. American, on the other hand, had to divest substantially to achieve the same result.

Delta and Northwest prospered throughout most of the deregulatory transition period. Both emerged from their regulated years in very strong positions, with conservative capital structures, low operating costs, and strong hub systems. Both built on those strengths steadily, achieving defensible competitive strategies characterized by a somewhat higher degree of geographic focus and a lower cost profile than American and United. Neither was or became diversified in this period.

Delta developed one of the strongest route systems in the regulatory period by building a classic hub operation in Atlanta. In 1980, it specifically stated that its strategy in deregulation was to strengthen and build hubs by linking them to small markets, adding that this was the "major source of our marketing strength."[41] Delta prospered through 1982 (while most other carriers encountered severe problems) by developing additional hubs in Dallas/Fort Worth and Cincinnati. Its success encouraged it to fund a major capital expenditure program to support expected rapid growth. During 1982 and 1983, Delta expended about $1.4 billion, chiefly for new B-767 and L-1011 aircraft and for new terminal facilities. Delta's long-term debt climbed from $362 million to $1.1 billion, resulting in a lofty debt-to-total-assets ratio of .72.

In 1983, Delta experienced its first loss in many years. As it tried to expand the scope of its service substantially, its strong competitive advantages were becoming diluted. Although Delta was able to defend its Atlanta hub against competitors setting up parallel operations, it faced American's dominance in Dallas/Fort Worth and United's dominance in Chicago, which led to declining yields. Moreover, its cost advantage began to diminish as it added substantial new debt to pay for the new aircraft and terminal facilities it needed to shift from a relative geographic focus to wide-market service.

Thus, Delta expanded out of a very defensible, lucrative, and sizable niche in which it had low costs and high entry barriers (stemming from a powerful, geographically focused, hub-based strategy). The further Delta moved from this sizable niche, the more it had to compete with other carriers that had other strong advantages (wide service or geographic focus in other regions). In the long run, it is doubtful that any wide-service carrier can achieve an unduplicable cost-leadership position, because economies of scale are limited in the industry. It is an open question whether Delta can match the wide-market, service-differentiated strategies of American and United, because, although it is a very skillful competitor, it is smaller and the market is relatively limited. In the long run, unless Delta can achieve wide-market service alongside American and United, it may have to limit its growth to the substantial and lucrative, but more limited, market segment it has served traditionally. If it remains in this highly profitable segment, it may have to adjust its corporate strategy later to shift its excess resources into diversification.

Northwest was a smaller airline that prospered under both regulation and deregulation. Like Delta, it emerged from regulation with a very conservative financial structure, lower operating costs, and a strong hub (centered in Minneapolis/St. Paul). It also had transpacific routes, drawing passengers from a gateway feeder system. Northwest prospered in deregulation by steadily building on these strengths. The carrier strengthened its route system by adding flights to Minneapolis/St. Paul and, later, by developing a smaller secondary hub in Chicago. It also slowly built its international flights and gateway feeder system, adding transatlantic flights with feed through Boston and New York. Unlike Delta, however, Northwest steadily added new aircraft and facilities without incurring massive, burdensome debt. It further increased the barriers to entry inherent in its hub system by differentiating itself with a highly focused advertising campaign that treated each city-pair as a separate segment, rather than targeting the broad market with a "top of mind" slogan campaign (meant to keep the brand name familiar).[42] This provided some protection against price competition eroding yields.

Northwest remained a single-business company under regulation and throughout the deregulation transition period. It also remained in a sizable niche, keeping geographically focused on the northern domestic tier of cities (serving selected domestic and international needs) and keeping costs low. There is substantial room to expand this lucrative and defensible niche at a measured pace. So long as Northwest has excellent prospects within the airline industry, with a substantial opportunity for long run growth and high profits, its single-business corporate strategy will continue to serve it well.

Several airlines had major difficulties in the deregulation transition period. Unlike the successful airlines, these carriers had problems creating defensible airline competitive strategies that were supported by adequate resources and matched by appropriate corporate diversification strategies. Eastern, Pan American, and Braniff tried to achieve wide-market, quality-service strategies without the necessary resources and strong multiple-hub systems. Continental and Western tried to maintain basically high-density, linear route structures. Tiger tried to position itself as an integrated transportation company with both air freight and truck operations (in addition to a rail car leasing subsidiary), but it neither created a defensible integrated air cargo operation capable of outcompeting freight forwarders that were integrating backward nor had the resources to fund its expansion in the face of a prolonged recession. As a result, all of these carriers hovered at or beyond the brink of bankruptcy. Several have been forced to sell their high-performing diversification ventures to pay for their airline losses.

Eastern entered the deregulatory transition period with several weaknesses. Years of losses had depleted its financial resources; its operating costs were high; and its labor relations were strained. Eastern's route system was exposed because it featured both a large hub in Atlanta (where Delta dominated the market) and many high-density, linear routes (primarily between Florida and the Northeast) that were exposed to competition from new entrants and established carriers seeking counterseasonal north–south routes.

Eastern's basic competitive strategy in deregulation was to drive toward a wide-market, quality-service stance. Eastern's attitude was summed up by its chairman, Frank Borman, who observed: "In a free market the only way to survive is from a position of leadership."[43] To support this, Eastern continued a massive reequipment program, purchasing twenty-two new jets in 1980, thirty-three in 1982 and 1983 (a very unstandardized fleet composed of two B-757s, eleven A-300s, sixteen B-727-200s, and four DC-9-53s), and seventeen jets in 1983 (thirteen B-757s and four A-300s). It also developed a diverse and broad route structure, with smaller hubs in Houston and Kansas City as well as the major hub in Atlanta.[44] The airline acquired Braniff's profitable South American routes and offered east–west transcontinental service with excess L-1011 and A-300 equipment.[45] In 1983, Eastern opened a route linking its main eastern operations with California, noting that this fulfilled a long-standing desire to link the West with the rest of its system.[46]

By 1984, Eastern's unrestrained drive toward wide-market service left it deferring debt payments, threatening bankruptcy, and trading 25 percent of its equity to its unions in return for the wage and work rule concessions necessary to remain solvent.[47] Eastern did not have the financial resources to fund a $2 billion reequipment program and to finance a major expansion in a period of intense competition and recession. Moreover, its route system was vulnerable to competition, because it did not rest on strong multiple hubs at which Eastern was the dominant carrier; hence, Eastern could not avoid constant price wars. Throughout this period, Eastern remained a single-business airline.

Even if Eastern could have achieved a wide-market strategy, it is questionable whether the market was large enough to support four or more major wide-market competitors (American, United, Delta, Eastern, and others). This strategic configuration probably would doom the carriers to constant capacity battles, and Eastern, as the weakest carrier, probably would face chronically low returns. A better strategy might have been to downsize into a defensible, geographically focused, service-oriented niche that was centered on the carrier's profitable and defensible routes. Eastern probably had the resources to achieve, consolidate, and vigorously defend a more limited airline competitive strategy, and high airline returns (in terms of return on investment, rather than absolute dollar amount) might have resulted. Any excess resources could have been channeled into strengthening its balance sheet and into a carefully thought-out diversification program. In this way, Eastern might have improved both its percentage and absolute dollar corporate returns.

Pan American experienced severe problems because it also attempted to move quickly toward a wide-market, quality-service strategy. The airline entered the late 1970s with a strong international route system, substantial and profitable diversification, and a relatively favorable capital structure. However, Pan American lacked a domestic feeder system and a fuel-efficient fleet of aircraft. In 1980, Pan American acquired National Airlines (after a vigorous bidding war) to remedy these deficiencies and to give it a broad market presence.

Pan American experienced severe problems and mounting losses in the aftermath of the National merger, because it kept the two systems largely separate and neither system had a defensible competitive advantage. The old Pan American international route system lacked the benefits of a significant domestic gateway system which would have fed captive east–west traffic into its international routes, and the old National system was largely composed of exposed north–south, high-density, linear routes. As competitors moved into this exposed system, yields plunged and losses accelerated.

In 1981, C. Edward Acker was hired to rescue Pan American. He replaced several former managers, refinanced and stretched the pressing debt burden, sold excess assets, and cut the work force and payroll (giving the employees, in return, 13 percent of the company's equity).[48] He also initiated major changes in the airline's route structure to provide a greater measure of integration and geographic focus. The carrier developed hubs in New York, Miami, Houston, Los Angeles, and San Francisco to protect the airline's traffic and to provide passenger feed to its main international routes.[49] In the following year, Pan American refined this system by significantly increasing the importance of its New York gateway, dropping its Houston gateway, and developing small international hubs in London, Frankfurt, and Tokyo.[50] The carrier also developed counterseasonal Caribbean routes.[51]

By 1984, Pan American appeared to have turned around, settling on a defensible, geographically focused, service-oriented strategy resting upon a strong gateway system that was feeding its international routes. In the earlier process of attempting to build a wide-market strategy, however, the airline sustained such massive losses that the corporation was forced to sell most of its very profitable diversification holdings. (It sold the Pan American Building for $300 million and Intercontinental Hotels for $500 million.) Faced with mounting airline problems, however, Pan American increased its profitable contract services diversification.

As with Eastern, Pan American's early attempted wide-market strategy seems to have been problematical. Even if the carrier had intended to integrate the old Pan American and National routes better, it probably did not have the resources to fund the start-up and development of a multiple-hub domestic system while developing a gateway feeder system for its extensive international routes unless it drew resources from its diversification ventures. Even if Pan American could have done this, it is very questionable whether the relatively limited market could have sustained five wide-market, service-differentiated carriers (American, United, Delta, Eastern, and Pan American). Had Pan American moved directly into the limited gateway feeder system it ended up with, it might have earned relatively high airline returns and accelerated its profitable diversification, instead of forfeiting it to avoid bankruptcy.

Braniff entered into deregulation in a position somewhat similar to that of Northwest. It had a favorable operating ratio and a strong hub operation (at Dallas/Fort Worth). Unlike Northwest, however, it had a high debt burden and a tradition of very high growth aspirations. Instead of building on its geographic and cost strengths at a pace it could support with its resources, Braniff sprinted toward large-carrier status by adding numerous domestic and international routes (table 5–8). During 1978, it added fourteen new aircraft, added east–west routes to counterbalance its north–south routes, and pursued a major international expansion.[52] Within a year, it encountered many of the problems that hurt Pan American: many routes were exposed to price competition; the route system was not well integrated; and the airline did not have the resources to fund the new routes' start-up period at adequate threshold frequencies. In 1981, Braniff tried to

Table 5–8
Net Change in Nonstop Markets, July 1978–July 1979

Airline	Net Change
Braniff	58
Trans World	23
Northwest	16
United	2
Pan American	−1
American	−2
Continental	−2
National	−3
Delta	−11
Eastern	−13
Western	−18

Source: Data presented by Elizabeth Bailey in a seminar at Harvard University in 1979.

restructure itself into a low-cost carrier and cut nearly all of its new services.[53] In 1982, however, its losses forced the carrier into bankruptcy.

As Braniff saw deregulation open new opportunities in the airline business, it reversed its corporate strategy and divested most of its diversification. At the time, a former senior corporate executive specifically linked Braniff's strategic direction to its perceived airline opportunities:

> By the time our initial efforts at diversification were coming to fruition and we were about to enter other areas, we heard the initial rumblings of deregulation, and renewed route availability began. We then moved our principal business resources and focus back to the airline.[54]
>
> The opportunity to invest in the airline refocused our efforts. We are better skilled in the airline business. The money needs of the airline are enormous. One 747 costs as much as a 1,000-room hotel.[55]

Braniff seems to have regarded itself as a strong competitor constrained by regulation. When unleashed, it expanded vigorously in several directions, divesting its diversification to raise capital for the airline.[56] Braniff differed from Northwest, however, in that it raced in several new directions, rather than building on its strengths, and it expanded at a pace that could not be supported by its resources. It might better have followed a strategy parallel to that pursued by Northwest: strengthening its already strong hub, opening complementary secondary hubs, and developing international routes protected by strong gateway feeder systems—all at a sustainable pace. Braniff's geographically focused niche probably would have permitted substantial long-run growth in the airline business. To the extent that Braniff reduced its poorly performing diversification to free resources for potentially lucrative airline opportunities, it had a reasonable corporate strategy.

In late 1983, the Pritzker family of Chicago (owners of the Hyatt Hotel chain and other businesses) purchased Braniff. The Prtizkers paid $20 million in cash to gain control over $94 million in Braniff assets and $325 million in tax benefits. The employees agreed to 30 to 40 percent pay cuts (with seniority maintained), lowering the cost per available seat-mile by about 25 percent. The new carrier positioned itself by targeting business travelers, offering a "first class experience at coach fares."[57] Although it is too early to judge the viability of this focused competitive strategy, one early assessment has suggested that the new Braniff may be repeating a key error of its predecessor by offering extensive rather than intensive service, thus leaving itself with an exposed route system and frequencies too low to attract service-sensitive (but price-insensitive) business travelers.[58] Historically, service has primarily meant schedule frequency and convenient departure times rather than marginal amenities, except on long-distance flights.[59]

Continental and Western encountered similar problems in the early part of the deregulation transition period. Both of these carriers carried forward from regulation very exposed route systems with large numbers of high-density, linear routes. With deregulation, both carriers increased those exposed routes and dropped smaller cities with feeder potential.[60] These actions would have been sensible under regulation but left both carriers without viable competitive strategies in the deregulated industry. Western, for example, generated about 25 percent of its traffic on its very exposed Hawaiian routes. Rather than moving into a more defensible posture, it opened even more exposed long-distance linear routes (without gateway or hub feeder systems) as diverse as Anchorage–London, Miami–London, Denver–London, and Minneapolis/St. Paul–Washington, D.C.

Both carriers experienced severe and rapid losses and twice tried to merge with each other. The merger, which the CAB turned down as anticompetitive, might have reduced competition and redundant operations, but it probably would not have strengthened the underlying route system nor prevented the losses. The huge resource drain caused by these exposed route systems forced both carriers to change management (Continental was taken over by Texas International, an aggressive regional carrier).

Surveying this period, both airlines' new managers came to the same conclusion. Continental's new owner noted that the market leaders, American and United, benefited from traffic feed, reservation system dominance, and marketing economies of scale, while many new carriers competed with low costs.[61] Continental had no niche but, rather, was "trying to be a miniature version of the industry giants."[62] Similarly, Western's new management noted:

During 1981 and 1982 it became apparent that the company's route structure, which had worked in an era of extensive government regulation of
the industry, was not well suited for successful operation's in a deregulated
environment. . . . Western operated primarily a point-to-point route structure serving medium haul, high density markets that lacked adequate feed
from beyond route segments. This structure provided no competitive advantage to Western against either new entrants having lower operating
costs, or existing trunklines and regional carriers having systems with substantial feed.[63]

A more recent Western Airlines chief executive wryly observed: "Merger
with Continental was their first plan, and their second plan was merger
with Continental."[64]

In attempting to reverse their huge losses, both carriers' new executives tried to restructure their route systems into hub configurations to
make them more defensible. Continental attempted to build a primary hub
in Denver and secondary hubs in Houston and El Paso, while slowly dropping high-density, linear services.[65] Western moved to reduce its size and
center its remaining operations on a Salt Lake City hub.[66] Both carriers
were severely depleted of resources by this time, however, and they had
problems developing traffic. This forced their management teams to focus
their strategies further in an effort to gain an edge.

Continental's new management saw the carrier's high cost structure as
the residual problem that prevented it from successfully developing a
niche. With continuing union resistance and mounting losses, Continental
declared bankruptcy in September 1983. It emerged from the reorganization
operating at about one-third of its former size and with a new, nonunion
work force earning salaries of about half of those that formerly prevailed.
The operating cost per available seat-mile was cut from about eight cents
to about six cents. These measures positioned the airline as a geographically focused, low-cost, discount (but full-service) carrier that expected to
earn profits by achieving high load factors. With the new strategy in place,
Continental moved to rebuild its operations steadily.[67]

Western's new management moved in a different direction to further
focus its airline. In 1983, it attempted to refine its segmentation strategy to
target the business travelers in its region, reasoning that this would decrease its dependence on price-sensitive leisure traffic.[68] The airline revised
its schedules and marketing programs to make it more attractive to its target segment.[69]

Continental carried forward its Type I diversification into this period
in a continuing effort to obtain transpacific routes. After the carrier successfully won the routes it sought, it moved promptly to sell its Pacific
hotel holdings, completing this in 1981. Continental entered into no significant new diversification in this period. Western, which was traditionally a

single-business airline, remained substantially focused on the airline business throughout deregulation.

The major problems these two carriers experienced in the deregulation transition period might have been avoided if their initial management teams had moved aggressively toward focused, defensible niches appropriate for deregulation, rather than continuing with old strategies appropriate for regulation. However, these two carriers (and National, which Pan American acquired) did not have the strong core hub systems and low costs that characterized the other smaller carriers—Delta, Northwest, and Braniff. To the extent that Continental and Western could shift and develop feasible and lucrative niches, it would have been sensible to devote resources to this effort rather than to diversify. However, in the not unlikely event that these carriers lacked the resources to build entirely new competitive strategies and route systems, they might better have retrenched into focused smaller niches centered on their profitable, defensible routes, channeling the freed-up resources into diversification. Failing that, they might have exited the industry entirely by becoming fully diversified.

Tiger, the large air freight carrier, experienced severe problems in its transition into deregulation. When air cargo was deregulated in 1977, Tiger rapidly attempted to become a fully integrated transportation company. It moved aggressively on three fronts. First, it sold its mortgage insurance company. Second, it expanded its air cargo operations by adding Anchorage, Charlotte, Atlanta, Houston, Dallas/Fort Worth, San Juan, and Cincinnati to its domestic route system and by acquiring Seaboard World Airways, an air cargo carrier with North Atlantic routes. Third, Tiger moved into trucking by acquiring Hall's Motor Transit (a large, less-than-truckload carrier, which in turn acquired Dohrn Transport Company) and Warren Transport (a specialized transporter of farm and heavy equipment). Although deregulation opened further air cargo opportunities, Tiger's management felt that there were natural constraints on its growth in the business. It believed that it could develop only about twenty-five terminals in the United States, because its large equipment could not serve small cities.[70]

By 1982, Tiger experienced such severe losses that it had to suspend its debt payments. The reasons for this likely stemmed from both intraindustry positioning problems and corporate problems. Although Tiger wanted to be a fully integrated transportation company, it did not actually integrate the strategies of its component companies. At the time of acquisition, Tiger was explicit that any truck line acquired had to be independently profitable and would be independently run. It regarded any tie-ins, such as establishment of a hub-and-spoke air/truck operation, as "gravy."[71] This left Tiger with a portfolio of parallel transportation businesses.

Tiger experienced severe competition on all fronts. The air cargo operation suffered from great overcapacity on the North Atlantic routes. Tiger's domestic operation experienced keen competition from former buyers (for example, Emery, Airborne, and UPS), which were integrating backward and carried with them long-standing customer loyalty based on product differentiation. These firms also ran more integrated multimodal operations. Tiger's trucking companies had mixed results, with Hall's broad, less-than-truckload operation losing money (even though the less-than-truckload market segment was more defensible than the truckload segment) and Warren's sharply focused operation running profitably. The rail car leasing subsidiary, which should have generated countercyclical cash flows (with recession cutting new purchases while the ongoing leases continued to pay out), suffered from the unusual temporary combination of prolonged recession and high interest rates. Beyond these problems, Tiger had entered deregulation with a very unfavorable debt burden that left little margin for error or for financing a major expansion. The company was forced to sell its strong rail car subsidiary, North American Car, and its other leasing and finance operations. This left Tiger with parallel air cargo and trucking operations and a small, multimodal distribution group.[72]

Tiger seems to have taken a portfolio approach to its corporate strategy, positioning itself with major holdings in both air freight and trucking to capture any intermodal freight shifts. This seems to have led to several strategic difficulties. Because the operations were not really integrated, Tiger could not build a viable, multimodal, wide-market, service-differentiated competitive strategy (similar to the freight forwarders) to give it a competitive advantage and to insulate it from price wars. Ironically, by 1984, both Flying Tiger and Hall's had moved strongly toward intermodal operations. Additionally, this strategy made Tiger much more vulnerable to economic cycles, as its air cargo and motor carrier businesses followed the same economic cycle. This increased its business risk, which suggests that lowering the company's financial risk (by reducing its debt burden) would have been sensible. As with Eastern, Pan American, and Braniff, Tiger might better have focused on consolidating a defensible integrated competitive position within the air cargo (and related trucking) industry, using the freed-up resources to strengthen its balance sheet and to fund a steady expansion building upon unduplicatable strengths.

Trans World experienced a very different but interesting transition into deregulation. The corporation entered deregulation with a chronically poorly performing airline and substantial diversification. Traditionally a weak wide-market carrier, Trans World attempted early in deregulation to develop hubs in New York, St. Louis, Chicago, Kansas City, and Pittsburgh.[73] It also opened counterseasonal north–south Florida routes.[74] However, with losses mounting as low-cost, nonunion competitors and traditional carriers with excess capacity moved into its many exposed routes, and as rising fuel prices rendered nearly half of its fleet obsolete, the corporation seems to have decided that the airline's prospects as a wide-market carrier were limited and that the brighter prospects of its diversified subsidiaries warranted increased resources.

Trans World had acquired Spartan Food Systems (a fast-food chain operation) and Century 21 (a real estate brokerage company) in 1979.[75] When it became clear in 1981 that the airline could not maintain its traditional wide-market position without massive investments, the corporation moved to accelerate its diversification and to downsize the airline steadily (table 5–9). In 1982, the airline rationalized and reduced its route structure to focus it on one domestic hub in St. Louis and an international gateway feeder system in New York.[76] By 1984, the airline's international operations were profitable, but its domestic operations remained unprofitable. Its competitive strategy was shifting toward increasing international operations, using a prestige image to target the high-service, price-insensitive segment of the market.[77]

In February 1984, Trans World spun off its airline (TWA). There appear to have been two reasons for this. First, severing the airline's financial links to the profitable diversification placed substantial pressure on its unions to grant wage and work rule concessions. This was crucial, because the airline's domestic operations were exposed to competition from low-cost carriers, and, although TWA's international operations were more insulated, Pan American and other high-service airlines with strong feeder systems were steadily reducing their costs.[78]

A second and probably more urgent reason for spinning off the airline was that Trans World Corporation's overall financial valuation was relatively low, because investors perceived it primarily as an airline (despite the fact that the preponderance of its earnings came from its diversification),

Table 5–9
Trans World Airlines' Domestic Market Share

Year	Domestic Market Share[a] (%)	Nonairline Revenue as a Percentage of Corporate Revenues
1979	10.4	31.6
1980	9.9	32.8
1981	9.3	33.3
1982	8.7	35.0
1983	8.4	36.0[b]

Source: Derived from SEC reports.

[a]Measured by TWA revenue passenger miles as a percentage of domestic major air carriers' revenue passenger miles.

[b]Theoretical calculation; TWA was spun off as an independent company, but Trans World Corporation retained links in 1983.

and airlines had much lower price-earnings ratios than those of the industries into which it had diversified. Moreover, the corporation was even more undervalued because the airline's chronically poor earnings canceled the strong earnings of the diversification. Because the corporation's stock price suffered from a lower price-earnings ratio and lower earnings than the diversification by itself would have warranted, and because the airline's assets had more earning power (thus value) in the hands of other carriers than they did in TWA's hands, the corporation was an attractive takeover target.

Predictably, Trans World attracted several takeover attempts. In 1983, Odyssey Partners (a small group of investment bankers) commissioned a major consulting firm study, which estimated Trans World's breakup value at about seventy dollars per share. At the time, the corporation's stock was trading for a fraction of that figure. In a proxy battle, the prospective purchasers received 23 percent of the votes.[79] Although the challengers lost, the handwriting was on the wall. Spinning off the airline was expected to result in a higher valuation for the high-performing conglomerate that remained, thus preventing a successful takeover. The stockholders were left with an independent airline, which was developing a limited, defensible market niche that (if properly managed) offered the prospect of high returns, and with a high-performing, higher-valued conglomerate. From the stockholders' perspective, the corporate strategy achieved positive results.

Evaluation

The airline industry's experience during its transition into deregulation confirms the usefulness of the strategic framework developed at the beginning of this book. The successful established carriers reduced their diversification as needed (or remained single-business firms) as their prospects for profitable growth in the airline business improved; and these prospects depended on their ability to build—upon existing strengths and resources—sound, defensible competitive strategies appropriate for the new environment. As a corporation, Trans World also achieved a degree of success in a different way: facing poor prospects in the airline industry, it downsized the carrier (which slowly moved toward a defensible niche) while it increased its high-performing diversification, ultimately spinning off the airline. The unsuccessful airlines, however, had problems in creating defensible airline competitive strategies (or exiting the industry) that were supported by appropriate corporate diversification strategies. By failing to fashion linked intraindustry competitive strategies (which were consistent with existing strengths and resources) and interindustry corporate strategies, the firms with high-performing diversification lost those businesses, and all either nearly or completely lost their airlines as well.

Notes

1. Meyer and Oster (1981) explore several of these factors.
2. Bruno interview (1979).
3. *Fortune*, 6/11/84.
4. U.S. Pub. L. No. 95-504 (1978).
5. Meyer (1976).
6. Meyer and Oster (forthcoming-a, ch. 11).
7. Ibid.
8. Meyer (1983).
9. Ibid.
10. AMR Corporation (1983a).
11. U.S. Pub. L. No. 95-504 (1978).
12. Ibid.
13. Meyer and Oster (forthcoming-a, ch. 11).
14. Meyer (1983).
15. U.S. Pub. L. No. 95-504 (1978).
16. Meyer and Oster (forthcoming-a, ch. 11) analyze the sources of the cost differential.
17. Caves (1962) and Fruhan (1972).
18. Meyer and Oster (forthcoming-a, ch. 11).
19. *Fortune*, 6/11/84.
20. Meyer and Oster (1981).
21. Ibid., ch. 8.
22. U.S. Pub. L. No. 95-504 (1978).
23. Meyer (1983, p. 38).
24. Porter (1980, ch. 2) identifies and analyzes these generic competitive strategies. Meyer (1983) has adapted Porter's (1980) discussion to explain the strategic transformation of the various airlines. In brief, under regulation, he identified Delta, Northwest, and National as focused cost leaders; American, United, and Trans World as service differentiators; Pan American, Braniff, Northwest and Trans World as international focusers; and Eastern, Western, and Continental as "stuck in the middle." Under deregulation, he identified Delta as a wide-market cost leader; Northwest, People Express, Pacific Southwest, Frontier, and Piedmont as focused cost leaders; and Eastern, Western, United, Pan American, and Republic as "stuck in the middle." This section updates Meyer's important findings and relates the intraindustry competitive dynamics to the overall corporate strategy problem.
25. Porter (1980, ch. 2); Meyer (1983).
26. Meyer and Oster (forthcoming-b).
27. Meyer (1981, ch. 8).
28. Meyer and Oster (forthcoming-a, ch. 11) point out that established carriers' management teams were often bloated with costly high-level personnel.
29. Meyer (1981, ch. 12) has suggested this as a potential motive for airline mergers.
30. The analysis which follows focuses on the major issues of intraindustry competitive positioning and corporate diversification. Most established carriers at-

tempted to lower their labor rates, upgrade their fleets, develop reservation systems and frequent-traveler programs, and similarly tune up their operations. These will be factored out of the analysis unless they are unusual or crucial to a carrier's strategy.

31. American Airlines (1980, pp. 8, 9).
32. Ibid.
33. *Business Week*, 4/23/84, p. 35.
34. AMR Corporation (1983).
35. *Fortune*, 6/11/84, pp. 38–51.
36. Casey interview (1979).
37. Ibid.
38. United Air Lines (1981, p. 7).
39. Bruno interview (1979).
40. Ibid.
41. Delta (1980).
42. Northwest (1982).
43. *Fortune*, 10/17/83.
44. Ibid; also Eastern (1983).
45. Eastern (1982); see also Meyer and Oster (1981, ch. 10).
46. Eastern (1983).
47. Ibid.
48. Pan American (1982).
49. Ibid.
50. Ibid.
51. Pan American (1983).
52. Braniff (1979).
53. Braniff (1981).
54. Background interview with a senior Braniff executive (1979).
55. Ibid.
56. The corporation kept Braniff Educational Systems because it was very small and was closely tied to the airline (Braniff executive interview, 1979).
57. *New York Times*, 2/26/84.
58. *Business Week*, 6/11/84.
59. This is the basis for the classic S-curve.
60. Meyer and Oster (1981, ch. 6).
61. *Business Week*, 3/19/84.
62. Ibid.
63. Western Airlines (1983, p. 1).
64. *New York Times*, 1/11/84.
65. Continental Airlines (1979).
66. Western Airlines (1981).
67. Texas Air Corporation (1983).
68. Western Airlines (1983).
69. Ibid.
70. Hoffman interview (1979).
71. Ibid.
72. Tiger International (1983).

73. Trans World Corporation (1980).
74. Ibid.
75. Trans World Corporation (1979).
76. Trans World Corporation (1982).
77. Trans World Corporation (1983).
78. *Business Week*, 3/19/84.
79. *Fortune*, 6/13/83.

6
Secondary Strategic Goals

The preceding chapters have presented and illustrated a framework for formulating corporate strategy that rests on the interaction between intraindustry and interindustry factors. The basic thrust of the framework is that a firm's interindustry corporate strategy should reflect an equilibrium among the firm's long-term prospects in its traditional business and its long-term possibilities in other industries. As regulation and deregulation shift a firm's prospects in its traditional business, it must make strategic adjustments.

This chapter steps back to analyze and evaluate several alternative explanations that are frequently cited to support major strategic moves. It assesses their theoretical soundness, evaluates their importance to the airlines, and highlights the role that secondary strategic goals can play. The temporal focus is placed the period from 1967 to 1978, when most airline diversification took place.

Several secondary strategic goals will be explored: enhanced utilization of tax benefits, reduction of cyclicality, financial speculation, joint operating and marketing economies, tying up of scarce resources, and selling of joint products and by-products. As before, the purpose of the discussion here is to provide in-depth guidelines for managers.

Investment Tax Credits

Utilization of investment tax credits is a frequently cited motivation for corporate diversification. The implicit reasoning is that the structure of the tax laws, particularly the investment tax credit provisions, create an incentive for marginally profitable companies to diversify in order to "purchase earnings" against which tax credits can be applied. This argument had potential relevance for the airline industry. Earlier chapters have shown that the regulated airline industry was characterized, in part, by fierce schedule frequency competition, equipment competition, and overrapid rates of equipment technical innovation. In response, many carriers loaded up on overhead and fixed charges while their profits eroded. The new equipment generated enormous investment tax credits and rapid depreciation allowances, leaving many carriers with huge, unutilized tax shelters.[1] By law, these shelters could be applied against the earnings of any member of the corporate family. Thus, a great incentive seemed to be created for buying earnings by diversifying. In effect, the cash flow from previously unsheltered earnings could be doubled.

Investment tax credits, first made available to firms in 1961, enabled firms to take a dollar-for-dollar credit off their tax payable. This credit initially was allowed to be 7 percent of a firm's capital investments in a particular year, but the credit was limited to offset no more than 50 percent of a firm's tax bill. Remaining credits could be carried forward for five years. These provisions were terminated by the Tax Reform Act of 1969, but credits could be gained for property acquired prior to termination if the property was placed in service on or before December 31, 1975.

The Revenue Act of 1971 restored the tax credit provisions, substantially as they stood before termination. The Tax Reduction Act of 1975 and the Tax Reform Act of 1976 raised the credit from 7 percent to 10 percent and instituted special rules for ships, airplanes, and trains. These rules significantly liberalized the maximum proportion of the tax bill against which credits from these capital assets could be applied, allowing them to be applied against 100 percent of the tax bill in 1977, 100 percent in 1978, 90 percent in 1979, 80 percent in 1980, 80 percent in 1981, and 90 percent in 1982 and thereafter. This provision came in response to an argument by air carriers (particularly United) that their chronic unprofitability in the preceding years had left them with insufficient tax bills against which they could apply the credits. The Tax Equity and Fiscal Responsiblity Act of 1982 reduced the maximum tax offset provision to 85 percent for 1983 and thereafter.

Leasing provided an important alternative for the carriers and removed much of the force of the argument that investment tax credit utilization constituted a major reason for diversification. In essence, if a firm expected not to be able to achieve enough profits to utilize its investment tax credits fully, it could arrange to have another, more profitable, firm own the asset and lease it back. The lease payments would be relatively low, since the lessor would pass on much of the investment tax credit and depreciation savings. Thus, according to Eastern's former vice-chairman, Charles Simons, investment tax credit utilization did not constitute a major incentive for Eastern's hotel venture, despite Eastern's chronically poor profitability. Eastern utilized aircraft investment tax credits as much as possible, and did leveraged lease purchases of airplanes to throw off the tax credits to those who could utilize them, in return for low interest rates. As an example of this arrangement, in 1979, Eastern arranged $100 million in fleet financing through fifteen-year leases at an effective interest rate of 5 percent. The equity was sold to blue-chip firms, such as Chase Manhattan Bank and Ford Finance Corporation.[2]

The same point was made by Martin Lynch, former vice-president for finance of Tiger International. He pointed out that Tiger's capital spending (that is, the lease versus buy decision) depended on its tax picture, and Tiger managed this rather than buying or selling companies for tax reasons. Thus, Tiger bought companies only for their earnings, although it was considered a plus if the shelter and earnings profiles matched.

Throughout most of the period, the IRS code required that leases have economic substance and not merely be conduits for tax benefits. The lessees generally lost the residual value of the asset (which could be substantial) and bore other minor disadvantages. The Economic Recovery Act of 1981 altered these provisions to allow substantially penalty-free transfer of the benefits through "safe-harbor" leases, which had little real economic substance. The Tax Equity and Fiscal Responsibility Act of 1982 removed the safe-harbor lease provisions. Thus, although leasing slightly disadvantaged firms for most of this period, it provided a close second-best alternative to owning for marginally profitable firms.

Table 6–1 gives an overview of the important role leasing played at the time in airline finance, comparing, on the one hand, the 1978 proportion of depreciation from owned equipment to total depreciation and amortization charges with, on the other hand, the mean ROE of respective carriers between 1973 and 1978—the period in which many of these commitments were made. The relationships that emerge are strong. Continental, Delta, National, Northwest, and Western, which did relatively little leasing, were relatively profitable and had little or no diversification. Braniff was strongly profitable but had to lease several airplanes to power its rapid expansion because it could not buy enough. United, even with substantial diversification, had to lease a portion of its fleet. American, with the poorly performing Americana Hotel chain and mixed 1978 prospects, leased a larger portion of its fleet. Tiger leased a substantial portion of its fleet, despite airline profitability, because it had very large tax shelters thrown off from its leasing subsidiary. Pan American, with the profitable Intercontinental Hotel chain but low overall earnings, leased a substantial portion of its fleet. Eastern and Trans World had the largest portion of leased aircraft in the group; they were among the lowest-performing firms.

Thus, as table 6–1 shows, leasing was a feasible and widely used alternative to buying a company for its earnings in order to utilize investment tax credits. However, there is one instance in which a company might be forced to purchase another to utilize tax credits. Because the lease versus buy decision depends on the expectation of earnings, a firm that had ex-

Table 6–1
Comparison of Asset Ownership and ROE (Airline Businesses Only)

Carrier	Depreciation of Owned Equipment as a Percentage of Depreciation and Lease Amortization, 1978	Mean ROE, 1973–1978 (%)
Western	90	15.4
Delta	100	15.1
Braniff	85	14.9
United	81	10.4
Flying Tiger	75	9.6
Northwest	100	9.2
Continental	100	8.1
American	75	7.1
National	100	6.2
Eastern	68	4.6
Pan American	80	3.0
Trans World	67	1.4

Source: Derived from CAB data.

pected high earnings but had unforeseen events reverse this expectation could be stuck with sizable investment tax credits and thus might be in a position in which buying a tax-paying company was a sensible move.

A literature search and case studies of four major carriers undertaken as part of this study revealed only two instances in which airlines stated that investment tax credits were significant incentives for diversification. Both of these instances were indeed situations in which unexpected and abrupt earnings drops occurred, and, significantly, in neither was the diversification a remedy to the investment tax problems.

Several officers of UAL stated that its need to utilize investment tax credits was an important reason for its major diversification in 1970. In the late 1960s, United was forced into a large-scale, economically premature equipment acquisition program, as the operating and competitive economics of wide-bodied aircraft forced airlines to purchase new equipment before old equipment was fully amortized or obsolete. Because of accelerated depreciation, UAL was recording virtually no profit (for tax purposes) and had little tax to offset with its mounting investment tax credits. In 1969, when United was reorganized into a subsidiary of UAL (a holding company), the firm had roughly $70 million in unused investment tax credits.[3] Concurrently, the major competitive route awards issued in the transpacific route case had a disastrous and long-lasting effect on United's profitability. Rexford Bruno, UAL's former senior vice-president–administration and finance, observed that, at the time, United was unable to utilize its investment tax credits because, under the prevailing rules, the investment tax credit could only be used to offset half of a firm's tax liability.[4]

In response to its problems, UAL moved on three fronts: it worked to change the investment tax credit laws, achieving this goal in 1977; it became a prime mover for deregulation to improve its profitability; and it diversified, purchasing Western International Hotels in 1970. In the years immediately following acquisition, however, Western International Hotels undertook a major building program that drove down earnings (accelerated depreciation and preoperating expenses were up-front deductions). Had investment tax credit utilization been the crucial reason for UAL's diversification, Western International probably would have been forced to curtail its deduction-generating major building programs and concentrate on generating maximum earnings from its already established properties. This would have been particularly likely because the Tax Reform Act of 1969 effectively placed a five-year time limit on tax credit utilization and, in addition, terminated the provision.

In 1969, Tiger cited investment tax credit utilization as an important reason for diversification. Tiger's 1969 annual report stated:

> We have substantial tax assets in the form of excess tax depreciation and investment tax credit carryforward. It is hoped that diversification will enhance our opportunity to use these sizable tax assets and to stabilize and increase earnings.[5]

Tiger had substantial tax shelters in 1969. It had just completed a $200 million acquisition of a new fleet of seventeen DC-8-63F aircraft. Because of accelerated depreciation and other tax deductions, Tiger was not required to pay federal income taxes in 1969. However, the Tax Reform Act of 1969 allowed only 20 percent of the investment tax credit carryforward to be applied in any one year, up to a maximum of 50 percent of the taxes payable. In 1969, Tiger had approximately $2 million per year that it could apply against taxes on future earnings, to a maximum of approximately $10 million. However, it had only an insignificant tax liability in the previous two years.[6] Hence, Tiger needed significant growth to utilize its tax credits, while it faced very uncertain prospects as its regulated business showed chronic losses and its military charter business fell off.

In choosing an acquisition, however, Tiger chose North American Car Company, a tax-shelter-generating rail car leasing company. Tiger felt that this firm fit so well with the airline, because of its stable and predictable earnings and cash-use characteristics, that it ignored the tax mismatch. As it turned out, the airline was unexpectedly profitable over the following several years and eventually needed all of the shelter provided by the leasing group. Hence, North American Car turned out to be correct from a tax point of view, but "for the wrong reasons," according to Tiger's former president, Thomas F. Grojean.[7]

Thus, United and Tiger provide the only two cases in which investment tax credit utilization provided a possible incentive for diversification.

In 1969, both firms suffered sharp reverses after a profitable period, and the termination provisions of the Tax Reform Act of 1969 added pressure. However, neither of these firms behaved in a way that was consistent with this diversification motive. UAL encouraged Western International Hotels to embark on a major expansion program, which lowered taxable earnings significantly; and Tiger purchased a leasing company, which generated tax shelters. Therefore, on balance, the evidence supports the conclusion that investment tax credit utilization did not constitute a major reason for diversification. At most, it may have prompted concerns that led firms to consider diversification that was undertaken for other, more compelling reasons.

Cyclicality

Reduction of cyclicality is another important reason often given for diversification. Cyclicality is generally regarded as a major element of risk, because it is always possible that a firm might go bankrupt during a severe economic downturn. The widely used measure of risk is the correlation of a firm's stock with market cycles (beta value). If the peaks and valleys are more pronounced and follow cycles roughly similar to those of the market, the stock is riskier, and a higher return must be offered to compensate for this risk. If a firm diversifies, the overall beta value of the firm will be the weighted average of the beta values of the component parts. The stock price, hence the cost of capital, will reflect the risk inherent in the overall beta value. Beyond this important conjoining effect, there is no evidence that diversification per se leads to an increase in the value of the firm, to a reduction in the cost of capital, or to better access to the capital markets.[8] However, the conjoining effect is of great potential importance to air carriers, as the industry is highly cyclical and firms carry high fixed-cost overheads.

Table 6–2 ranks the airlines by variance in ROE (airline operations only). This table fails to demonstrate a strong association between earnings variance and diversification, although it appears that it might have been a contributing cause in a few instances. Delta, with no diversification, had a medium degree of variance relative to the industry, except that its earnings were more stable between 1969 and 1973. National had a very mixed record of earnings stability. In two periods, including the crucial period 1969–1973, National ranked well below average in earnings stability, yet it did not diversify. Northwest, with relatively little earnings variance, did not diversify. Western, with no diversification, had relatively volatile earnings, particularly between 1964 and 1973. This strongly suggests that, with the

Table 6–2
Airline Ranking by Standard Deviations of ROE

	1959–1963			1964–1968			1969–1973			1974–1978		
Carrier[a]	Std. Dev.	ROE (%)	Carrier[a]	Std. Dev.	ROE (%)	Carrier[a]	Std. Dev.	ROE (%)	Carrier[a]	Std. Dev.	ROE (%)
CO	2.3	8.1	UA	3.1	11.5	PA	1.8	(7.3)	BR	2.1	14.9
UA	2.6	5.9	AA	3.4	15.9	CO	2.4	5.7	NW	2.1	9.2
AA	3.8	8.6	NA	3.6	22.4	DL	2.5	15.6	FT	3.0	9.6
NW	4.6	9.8	NW	3.6	22.4	NW	2.8	7.9	NA	3.6	6.2
BR	5.1	4.3	PA	4.3	1.6	BR	4.5	13.4	DL	4.0	15.1
PA	5.4	9.0	DL	4.7	23.8	FT	5.0	19.6	AA	6.8	7.1
DL	6.4	12.8	WA	5.6	17.6	AA	6.6	1.0	WA	7.1	15.4
NA	7.1	11.9	BR	6.9	9.0	NA	6.9	7.9	CO	9.4	8.1
WA	7.3	13.3	TW	7.1	15.8	EA	7.3	(1.4)	UA	10.1	10.4
FT	14.0	(3.3)	CO	8.7	20.6	UA	8.0	4.8	EA	12.2	4.6
TW	24.4	2.3	EA	13.1	5.0	WA	11.4	4.5	TW	15.4	1.4
EA	30.1	5.0	FT	14.1	11.7	TW	12.3	2.8	PA	21.7	3.0
Aggregate	4.3	5.8		4.6	19.3		2.1	2.9		6.8	6.7

Source: Derived from CAB data.

[a] AA = American Airlines; BR = Braniff; CO = Continental; DL = Delta; EA = Eastern; FT = Flying Tiger; NA = National; NW = Northwest; PA = Pan American; TW = Trans World; UA = United Airlines; WA = Western Airlines.

possible exception of Northwest, the nondiversifiers were motivated to re-main single-business firms by their profitability and airline industry pros-pects, rather than by earnings stability.

Continental had a very mixed record, with very stable earnings be-tween 1969 and 1973 and very unstable earnings in the periods 1964–1968 and 1974–1978. Although it first diversified in a period of unstable earn-ings, it continued and expanded its program in a period of very stable earn-ings. An earlier chapter demonstrated that Continental's diversification was route-related, and this evidence confirms that view. Braniff had only moderately stable earnings in 1964–1968; between 1969 and 1973, earnings were relatively stable; and they were very stable between 1974 and 1978. Braniff's diversification came in a period of earnings stability; hence, Bran-iff's diversification also does not appear to be related to earnings variance. Interview evidence confirmed this.[9]

Eastern had severe variance in its returns. The source of this variance, however, was Eastern's very low returns during several bad years, and, at best, it matched the aggregate return in other years. Therefore, Eastern's problem was not really earnings variance but, rather, periodic disastrous years. Thus, although earnings variance was significant, it was not the source of Eastern's problems but, rather, a manifestation.

Charles Simons, Eastern's former vice-chairman, explicitly stated that Eastern's prime reason for diversifying was to gain routes. He then noted that Eastern was also interested, though to a much lesser extent, in obtain-ing countercyclical effects from its diversification. Although the Puerto Ri-can hotel, the Dorado Beach, was located at one of Eastern's major destina-tions, it was so popular that it was not cyclical. The Mauna Kea and the Dorado Beach were among the very best hotels in the world; therefore, they were usually full. In addition, Eastern expected the Mauna Kea to draw business from Japan as well as from the U.S. mainland. The Cerromar, how-ever, which was basically a convention hotel and was built later, was very cyclical.[10]

Pan American had very stable earnings in the first three periods, and in 1969–1973 it had the most stable earnings of any of the firms. Its problem was that its earnings were stable at a subnormal level, which probably is why it diversified (by steadily developing Intercontinental Hotels) despite its low earnings variance.

American's earnings variance was very similar to, or lower than, those of the four nondiversifying firms, yet American diversified actively. In the period immediately preceding American's major entry into the hotel busi-ness, it ranked second in earnings stability. In the following periods, span-ning 1969 to 1978, it had only moderate variance, but it substantially in-creased its diversification. Therefore, earnings variance does not seem to have been an important motivation for American's diversification.

United had very little earnings variance from 1959 to 1968, but then had relatively unstable earnings in its period of diversification, 1969 to 1978. This seeming association was supported by interviews. Rexford Bruno, former senior vice-president of UAL, cited a high degree of cyclicality of earnings as one of the causes of UAL's diversification;[11] and Irvin Williamson, former vice president–finance of UAL, observed that in 1969, when it embarked on diversification, UAL was considered by institutional investors to be a cyclical trading stock.[12] An examination of the record reveals that the incremental variance of United's returns over that of the aggregate industry primarily stemmed from the 1970 transpacific route awards, a 1973 debenture exchange, and 1978 deregulation. Thus, there is some evidence that cyclicality was a secondary motivation for United's diversification.

Trans World had a substantial earnings variance. Like Eastern, most of this variance was caused by the firm's poor performance in a few years, although it occasionally outperformed the industry. There is only weak associative evidence that earnings variance caused the early Hilton International diversification, although cyclicality was not mentioned prominently by Trans World or by the press as a reason for that acquisition. In 1980, however, Trans World was explicit that the desire to reduce cyclicality played an important part in its later acquisitions:

That we were able to remain profitable in 1980 despite an adverse economy was mainly because of the success of two key elements of our strategy. . . . The first was a moderation of the airline's traditionally magnified vulnerability to the cycles of the airline industry. . . . The second was that in 1980 the corporation enjoyed full-year contributions from a total of four subsidiaries in non-airline service businesses, including two that were acquired in 1979 as part of the further broadening of our nonairline earnings base.

In 1970, our only source of nonairline income was Hilton International, whose contribution of $15.3 million in pre-tax profit was far outweighed by the airline's deficit, resulting in a corporate net loss of $93.2 million. In 1975, although Hilton International had by then been joined by Canteen Corporation, their combined contribution of $34.2 million in pre-tax profits was still more than offset by the airline's losses, and we experienced a corporate net loss of $91.9 million.

In the 1980 recession, however, our four nonairline subsidiaries contributed a total of $114.6 million in pre-tax profits, which more than offset the airline's loss (excluding the extraordinary gain), and the corporation as a whole achieved a profit.[13]

Although it is clear from the preceding statement that Trans World diversified, in part, to reduce the effects of the airline's cyclicality, it was also broadening its nonairline profile in response to its airline prospects. It is likely that during the 1970s, Trans World initially was motivated more by cyclicality; later (as fuel prices made much of the fleet obsolete and the airline's competitive prospects dimmed), it was motivated more by its relatively unfavorable airline prospects.

Tiger experienced very severe earnings variance in the decade preceding its initial diversification. This variance was substantial and fluctuated widely around a respectable mean ROE. In 1968, the year immediately preceding Tiger's initial diversification, Tiger earned a very low return. In each of the following two periods, 1969–1973 and 1974–1978, its earnings variance appeared to be modest. Because of an abrupt drop in ROE at the breakpoint in 1974, however, the ten-year series exhibits far more variance. Furthermore, in the period of diversification, Tiger's airline exhibited strong ROE and growth. This suggests a strong association between Tiger's extreme earnings variance and its diversification.

Interview evidence suggests that cyclicality was a strong cause of Tiger's diversification. Tiger's chairman, Wayne Hoffman recalled that, in 1970, he wanted an acquisition with stable earnings because he felt that the airline was very cyclical.[14] Thomas Grojean, Tiger's former president, noted that his firm believed that North American Car Company fit the airline so well because of its stable and predictable earnings that Tiger ignored the tax mismatch between the firms.[15] North American Car had a fleet of about 50,000 railroad cars, with about 88 percent on continuing long-term leases at any time. Thus, only 12 percent of the revenues were exposed in any year; in lean years, earnings would merely flatten. Tiger acquired the Investor's Mortgage Insurance (IMI) company for similar reasons. IMI's revenues were very stable; because IMI wrote long-term contracts, only about 15 percent of its revenues were exposed each year. In a recession, Tiger expected the IMI's earnings would merely flatten, not plunge.

Mr. Grojean explicitly confirmed that earnings stability was a prime attraction in considering purchase of both firms. He explained:

> It was necessary to join North American Car to the airline because the airline alone was too cyclical. It would make money, then lose money. If it paid out the flush years' earnings as dividends, there would not be anything to draw on in lean years when needed.[16]

In this view, leasing could perform a sort of internal banking function, with the rate of equipment acquisition (cash outlays), if necessary, varying inversely with the airline's cash needs. In an economic downturn, the demand for new leased equipment was expected to fall, so net cash outflow for new equipment would fall, and the leasing group would become a strong

Table 6–3
Correlations of ROE within Major Diversified Carriers,
1972–1978

Carrier	Correlation
Tiger International	
Airline–leasing	.0968
Trans World	
Airline–hotels	.5908
Airline–Canteen	(.0063)
Hotels–Canteen	.5597
American	
Airline–subsidiaries	.5054
United	
Airline–hotels	.5362
Airline–insurance	.8901
Hotels–insurance	.4582
Pan American	
Airline–hotels	.7275

Source: Derived from SEC reports.

cash generator. At the same time, the airline would become a strong cash user. The opposite was expected to occur in prosperous periods.[17]

Thus, the evidence shows that cyclicality was not strongly associated with corporate diversification in most cases. There were three important exceptions, however. First, there was both statistical and case study evidence that earnings variance was a factor in United's diversification. Second, both Trans World's early and most recent diversifications appear to have been only marginally related to cyclicality, whereas its diversification in the middle and later 1970s appears to have been strongly related to its chronic cyclicality. Finally, Tiger's initial diversification in the early and mid-1970s also appears to have been strongly motivated by its desire to reduce its cyclicality. Table 6–3 confirms these findings. During the 1972–1978 period, Trans World's Canteen returns and Tiger's leasing returns were relatively uncorrelated with the respective airline's returns. The other non-airline subsidiaries' returns were much more correlated with the respective airlines' returns.

Financial Speculation

The possibility that corporate diversification strategies were undertaken simply as financial speculations is a relatively straightforward proposition.

The financial markets are not always perfect, and variations in rates of return on short-term investments can be observed. These variations can be rooted in long-term trends, such as changes in tastes or technology, but they also can be rooted in short-term considerations, such as the necessity to divest because of antitrust regulations or the necessity to sell to avoid estate-tax difficulties.[18]

The air carriers entered into a few ventures that had elements of financial speculation. Financial speculation is defined here as buying a company simply because it was undervalued as a result of such factors as antitrust regulations and bankruptcy. It is important to mark the difference between financial speculation and more general diversification, which seeks to add a business with desirable long-term prospects.

Three ventures appear to have elements of financial speculation: UAL's 1975 acquisition of GAB Business Services, Tiger's 1975 acquisition of the Investors Mortgage Insurance Company, and American's 1977 purchase of oil and gas interests from the Republic Corporation. All three firms picked up their ventures at bargain prices.

In 1975, United purchased GAB Business Services, an insurance adjustment firm. This was a year in which United saw the CAB fail to renew the temporary capacity limitation agreements that had enabled the firm to do well in 1974. In this year, also, United posted a loss. These factors prompted United's parent, UAL, to search for another acquisition. In searching for an acquisition after absorbing Western International Hotels, UAL saw the natural course to be staying close to travel—most obviously, more hotels. Since it already had Western International, which was developing the high-quality end of the market, the alternative was a chain of less-expensive hotels. It was felt, however, that this would lead to problems, because mixing up different grades of hotels would hurt Western International. The other alternatives in travel were also problematic. Almost the only other major travel-related possibility was a rent-a-car company, but there were no companies left to acquire; Hertz was owned by RCA, National by Household Finance, and ITT could not come to terms with UAL for Avis.[19]

Given this background, financial considerations dominated the search. The new criteria were (1) consistency of earnings; (2) return on investment; (3) amount of taxable earnings: (4) noncapital-intensity—because hotels and airlines are capital-intensive; and (5) capital turnover—because UAL's rate of capital turnover was roughly one time per year. There also was a set of instinctive negatives—that is, "I don't want to be in that industry." Finally, UAL did not want to get involved in a turnaround that might take management attention away from the airline or the holding company.[20]

UAL conducted its search for new acquisitions at the staff level. Besides analyzing the travel business, it undertook a proactive in-depth look at opportunities in food service, because it had some knowledge or expertise in that business. Other possibilities were examined more randomly, such as when brokers brought proposals to UAL.[21]

GAB Business Services was brought to the attention of UAL's chairman by a friend. Although it was small, it appeared attractive because it met all of UAL's financial criteria for an acquisition—and it was available. GAB Business Services, which was owned by a group of insurance companies, primarily provided insurance adjustment services at peak load times. It was the object of an antitrust action and consequently was divested in 1973, when it was sold to a group of venture-capital investors. Two and a half years later, in October 1975, it was sold to UAL. The purchase price was low, because GAB had little cash.[22] Thus the record shows that the opportunity for financial speculation merely shaped the direction UAL took, but the causes and the intention to diversify preexisted.

Investors Mortgage Insurance Company was offered to Tiger by an investment banking firm; it had been seized as collateral in the bankruptcy of the former parent firm. There is no evidence that Tiger was actively seeking an acquisition at that time, but in interviews, the officers of Tiger strongly emphasized that this firm "fit" because of its earnings stability, cash-user nature, and unsheltered earnings.[23] Thus, it appears that this acquisition was motivated by a combination of financial speculation and satisfaction of preexisting needs.

American's 1977 purchase of the oil and gas interests of the Republic Corporation also indicates mixed motivations. This was a forced divestiture: the Federal Reserve Board did not want bank holding companies to own nonbank businesses. Interview evidence strongly suggests that American's management perceived that regulation had created the conditions for this venture by foreclosing American's opportunities in the airline business.[24] This view was confirmed by reference to the statistical record. In an interview, however, American's chairman, Albert Casey, emphasized the risk-free nature of the investment, which was paid by a nonrecourse loan.[25] Therefore, it appears that although CAB regulation had created important elements of the conditions that brought American to make this acquisition, financial speculation played a role in shaping the direction of diversification.

Thus, in all three instances, it appears that the conditions that made the firms receptive to further diversification were caused by other factors. The bargain prices of the acquired firms seems merely to have pulled diversification in a particular direction. This view is bolstered by interview evidence, which suggests that these firms were constantly having deals brought to them by outside parties.[26] Hence, other, more basic factors explain which firms were disposed to accept offers, while financial speculation helps explain which offers were accepted by the firms that were so disposed.

Joint Economies

Some people have argued that corporate diversification is undertaken to gain specific joint economies. Joint operating economies can be sought through such measures as shared facilities and exchanges of personnel or technology. Similarly, joint marketing gains can be sought through such measures as cross-feeding traffic and shared advertising.

There is no evidence that airline corporate diversification took place to gain joint operating economies, and interview evidence shows that only minor gains of this sort took place. There is some evidence that a desire to cross-feed traffic motivated some diversification, particularly on long-haul routes to developing regions—such as Braniff's routes to South America and Continental's route to Micronesia—but these are special cases and were really a form of Type I diversification or regulatory-related route development.

The role that the desire to cross-feed traffic on developed routes played in motivating diversification (particularly into hotels) was noted by Lynn P. Himmelman, former chairman of UAL's executive committee and UAL director (who was an executive of Western International Hotels at the time). He observed that there was an attitude in the airline industry that unless an airline could assure passengers accommodations, it could not get passengers.[27] If this was an element of the initial interest in diversification, however, it was quickly recognized as a specious argument.

Harry Mullikin, chairman of Western International Hotels, affirmed his firm's independence of United's strategy. He noted that the potential for United to feed people into Western International Hotels is "far less than people think." On any flight, half of the people are going home, and one-fourth are visiting friends; hence, only the remainder are potential hotel customers, and they usually have made other arrangements by the time they fly. Furthermore, these hotels are very popular on their own. The New York Plaza, for example, has 800 rooms and guests stay an average of four nights. Therefore, there are 200 rooms available on any particular day, and Western International turns down several times that number of requests per day for this hotel.[28]

Eastern also did not want to tie its hotels closely to its airline business in an operational sense. Its former vice-chairman, Charles Simons, reasoned that Eastern carried roughly 40 percent of the air traffic to Puerto Rico, but that its hotels offered less than 1 percent of the island's hotel rooms. Therefore, he felt that Eastern could "get killed" by the other hotels if it tried to channel traffic to its own hotels. Beyond this, he felt that the Dorado Beach was of such high quality that it was usually filled anyway. The Cerromar, which was a convention hotel, was somewhat tied to Eastern's charter department. Since Eastern had no routes to Hawaii, no operational ties existed between the Mauna Kea and the airline.[29]

Thus, a desire for joint gains does not appear to have been a major motivating factor in airline diversification. With the exception of shared computer systems, there were no substantial operating economies, and in some cases diseconomies outweighed potential economies. Although a desire for cross-feeding traffic may have helped push diversification interest toward hotels, such cross-feeding was generally not feasible and was immediately so recognized by those involved in the ventures. Therefore, it probably would not have contributed a reason for continued diversification beyond an initial curiosity. The two seeming exceptions, Braniff and Continental, were probably really responding to route development incentives, and they are not relevant examples.

Scarce Resources

Diversification that is undertaken to tie up a scarce resource or to avoid exposure to price rises of an important cost factor is a potential strategic motivation. Under regulation, air carriers were particularly vulnerable to sharp price increases in the factors of production, because there was a regulatory lag in passing on cost increases. Fuel cost increases were especially problematic, because they were large and sharp; labor cost increases, though substantial, came only at intervals and thus were easier to pass along. Unavailability of fuel also posed problems: because of the S-curve effect, a carrier with an assured fuel supply could swiftly increase market share more than proportionally as competitors were forced to cut back their schedules.

Instances of diversification to tie up a scarce resource or to avoid exposure to price rises of an important cost factor are rare in this group of firms. American's purchase of oil and gas interests suggests the former motivation; and Tiger has argued that the latter motivation was partially responsible for its diversification.

Albert Casey, chairman of American Airlines, noted that the oil and gas business, unlike the airline business, is neither labor-intensive nor fuel-intensive. He also felt that being in the oil and gas business gave American Airlines an inside track for airline fuel through its trading activities. This was quite important for American because, like other airlines, it was badly hurt by fuel price hikes and scarcity. At the time the purchase of the oil and gas interests was negotiated, American faced expiration of a low-priced supply contract that had been negotiated with Texaco just before the oil embargo and subsequent price rises. This contract supplied half of American's needs and had directly contributed roughly $35 million of American's after-tax earnings.[30]

AA Energy Corporation was set up in 1977 as a closely affiliated firm to manage and develop American's oil and gas properties. The top overseer of the oil and gas operations was American's senior vice-president, who is also in charge of flying and buying oil and gas for the airline. Mr. Casey chose him for this dual task to closely tie in the companies.[31] This suggests that American was motivated, in part, by a desire to secure a source of fuel supply. However, other evidence, discussed in previous sections, suggested that American's perceived lack of opportunities and its subnormal airline returns created the conditions for this diversification, while integrative and speculative opportunities merely shaped the direction.

Tiger had argued in the Air Carrier Reorganization Investigation that its diversification enabled it to insulate itself against the escalating labor costs of the airline industry. Although its choice of North American Car and Investors Mortgage Insurance tends to bolster this view, interview evidence suggests that this was not an important factor; none of the officers of Tiger mentioned this as a reason for diversification. More important, Tiger convincingly argued in 1974 that, if permitted, it would have no trouble passing on factor cost increases to its price-insensitive air freight customers.[32] Therefore, it seemed that the real problem posed by escalating labor costs for Tiger was that CAB rate regulation did not allow it to pass on high costs. In this sense, it was at root a regulatory problem.

By-Products and Overhead

Diversification that is undertaken to sell a by-product or to spread the overhead of a segment of the business rests upon marginal cost considerations. If a facility has a fixed minimum efficient scale size and the carrier can use only a portion of the capacity, it can be profitable to sell the products of the remaining capacity to others. Similarly, unutilized by-products can be sold to others for marginal gains. If sales to others can absorb the entire overhead of the operation and the producer gets the goods or services it requires at marginal cost, then the firm can potentially increase its profits.[33]

There is substantial evidence that most firms sold by-products and sold services to spread the overhead of underutilized departments. Most airlines undertook some maintenance and catering for other airlines; several sold space on their computer reservations systems; and several sold simulator time. These were relatively incidental, however, and did not have an important impact on earnings.

American sold the highest proportion of this sort of business to outside firms. Its Sky Chefs subsidiary consistently showed an operating profit and was involved in a variety of activities, including airport dining rooms, coffee shops, bars and cocktail lounges, flight catering for American and other carriers, retail shops, and similar activities. At peak, roughly half of its revenue stemmed from sales to customers other than American Airlines, although it sold its services to more than thirty airlines in all. At the time, nearly one-quarter of its revenue came from services other than in-flight catering. However, American's development of Sky Chefs' nonairline business followed much the same development pattern as that of Americana Hotels: in the early and mid-1970s, when American's airline business was suffering and its airline prospects looked dim, Sky Chefs substantially increased its business with other firms, both within and outside the airline industry, following a typical Type II diversification pattern.

By 1978, deregulation had opened new opportunities for American in the airline business, and Sky Chefs cut back so that it served only airports and airlines. Of the thirteen airports at which it operated food or beverage facilities, all except Denver and Portland were on American's scheduled route system. Of its twenty-five flight kitchen facilities, all but Denver, Hilo, and Portland were on American's scheduled route system. Of its nine airport retail shops, all but Portland were located in American's scheduled route system. Mr. Casey considered Sky Chefs to be closely allied with the airline, and he believed this gave American Airlines a chance to control the quality and service of the product.[34]

Thus, the experience of American in developing Sky Chefs is consistent with the findings of the preceding chapters. American started Sky Chefs to serve its airline. When opportunities in the airline business seemed to be foreclosed by regulation, however, American expanded Sky Chefs and it took on a life separate from the airline. When airline opportunities again became available with deregulation, Sky Chefs was reduced in scope. Several other airlines sold services to outside firms, but this was rather marginal in most instances.

Evaluation

The evidence strongly suggests that the alternative strategic goals examined in this chapter were secondary, at best, to the needs of firms to construct strategies that equilibrated their long-term prospects in their traditional and alternative businesses. The importance of the first alternative strategic goal, which concerned investment tax credit utilization as a diversification incentive, is largely unsupported by the evidence. Leasing was a feasible and widely used remedy for unprofitable firms that expected to remain so. Only when firms expected to be profitable and had this expectation abruptly and unexpectedly changed could a case be made for diversification to utilize investment tax credits. It was shown that only UAL and Tiger in the late 1960s possibly fit this description. However, the subsequent diversification behavior of both firms cast doubt on the significance of this strategic motive.

A stronger case could be made for the proposition that diversification was undertaken by some carriers to reduce cyclicality. UAL's record displayed some association between cyclicality and diversification, and Tiger's and Trans World's records during the 1970s showed strong evidence that cyclicality was a motivating factor. For most carriers, however, no association could be established. Therefore, although there was support for the significance of this motivation in two instances, the overall association was not so strong or systematic as that established between intraindustry competitive prospects and interindustry diversification.

There were a few cases of financial speculation in which airlines purchased firms because they were selling for bargain prices. The evidence established, however, that the speculating airlines were already looking for acquisitions. Therefore, the bargain nature of the acquisition appears to have determined the choice of firm but not to have motivated or caused (in a strict sense) the decision to diversify.

No substantial evidence could be found to support the notion that diversification was undertaken to gain specific joint operating economies; any gains were found to be incidental and often were more than offset by diseconomies. The parallel idea—that joint marketing gains were sought through such measures as cross-feeding traffic—was shown to be often a fallacious notion and was so recognized by most carriers. It was found, however, that American's and UAL's initial interest in possibly cross-feeding traffic had a role in sparking their interest in diversification, although later carrier behavior clearly showed that this was not an important cause of the diversification.

Evidence shows that diversification to tie up a scarce resource or to avoid exposure to price rises of an important cost factor was, at best, a minor consideration in American's purchase of the Republic Corporation's oil and gas interests. Evidence showed, however, that profitability and growth problems attributed by the carrier's management to regulation prompted American's actual decision to diversify further. The fit between the firms merely shaped the direction of that diversification.

Diversification that was attempted to sell a by-product or to spread the overhead of a segment of the business was found to be a common but not very significant business practice. Nearly every firm undertook some activities of this sort, but in most cases they were not very important. Where substantial business was developed outside the industry, the diversification waxed and waned in accordance with the more basic strategic considerations developed in earlier chapters. Thus, with the exception of a few isolated instances, the diversification goals analyzed in this chapter were secondary to the underlying need to respond to shifting intraindustry competitive prospects with an evolving interindustry corporate strategy.

Notes

1. Bruno interview (1979); Hoffman interview (1979).
2. Simons interview (1979).
3. See UAL (1969).
4. Bruno interview (1979).
5. See Tiger (1969, p. 4).
6. Ibid.
7. Grojean interview (1979).
8. See Myers (1976) and Van Horne (1977).
9. Background interview with a senior Braniff executive (1979).
10. Simons interview (1979).
11. Bruno interview (1979).
12. Williamson interview (1979).
13. Trans World Corporation (1980, p. 4).
14. Hoffman interview (1979).
15. Grojean interview (1979).
16. Ibid.
17. This failed to occur during the recession of the early 1980s, when a protracted downturn was coupled with unusually high interest rates.
18. See Sherer (1970, pp. 114–116). Also, Hindley (1970) found, in a comparison of firms subjected to takeover attempts with similar firms not so subjected, that the ratio of book value to market value of firms subjected to takeover attempts was one and a half times larger than the ratio of book value to market value of firms not subjected to takeover attempts.
19. Bruno interview (1979).
20. Ibid.
21. Ibid.
22. Ibid.
23. Hoffman interview (1979) and Grojean interview (1979).
24. Casey interview (1979).
25. In 1975, the year before American acquired it, this business earned $6.5 million, and it had oil and gas reserves valued, in 1976, at over $100 million. American purchased the business for $60 million and at no risk; in return, it shared the benefits with Republic through a unique "come back in" deal designed by Mr. Casey. American bought the properties for approximately $60 million, of which about $15 million was equity and $45 million was debt. When the bank loan is repaid in full and American recovers its entire investment with 10 percent per annum interest, Republic will have the right to receive 50 percent of the net cash flow derived from any remaining assets. Formally, this is represented by a warrant entitling Republic Corporation to acquire an issue of the preferred stock of the AA Development Corporation (Casey interview, 1979).
26. Hoffman interview (1979), Grojean interview (1979), Simons interview (1979), Bruno interview (1979). See Byrnes (1980) for supporting case study evidence.
27. Himmelman interview (1979).

28. Mullikin interview (1979).
29. Simons interview (1979).
30. Casey interview (1979).
31. Ibid.
32. Tiger (1974a).
33. In practice, many airlines have weakened their entry barriers by this practice. See Chapter 5.
34. Casey interview (1979).

7
The Implementation of Corporate Strategy: Determinants of Airline Diversification Profitability

A successful company not only must formulate a sound corporate strategy, it also must skillfully implement the strategy. The preceding chapters of this book developed and illustrated a framework for formulating corporate strategy which provided guidelines for *when* companies should diversify. Here we will examine the further question of *how* companies should and should not diversify. We will analyze the airline industry's experience to distill the determinants of the profitability of their diversification ventures, providing important clues for managers who have chosen to diversify their firms.[1]

Table 7–1, which deals with the seven-year period 1972–1978, shows that the diversification ventures can be sorted for convenience into two groups according to mean ROE, with a break-point occurring at roughly 5 percent. Both of Trans World's nonairline businesses, Hilton and Canteen, were very strong performers. Both of Tiger's businesses, leasing and mortgage insurance, posted high returns. Pan American's Intercontinental Hotels chain was profitable. (Pan American's contract services figures were not broken out in reports of this period.) UAL's Western International Hotels posted only a moderate mean ROE; this statistic is misleading, however, because the large front-end, preoperating expenses and accelerated depreciation of the strong building program it undertook in the early and mid-1970s pulled down its ROE. UAL's GAB Business Services was in the process of being turned around by Mr. Williamson during this period; hence, its mean ROE statistic is also probably misleading.

Several businesses were substandard performers during this period (both by absolute standards and relative to other firms in their industries in this group of firms), underperforming even municipal bonds. The ROE of American Airline's Americana hotel chain could not be disaggregated from published information, but it is obvious from its chronically large reported losses that it had a large negative ROE. (American's Sky Chefs subsidiary had consistent profits, but since well over 50 percent of its business was done with American Airlines, this could reflect transfer pricing policies;

Table 7–1
Comparison of Businesses along Several Dimensions, 1972–1978

Business[a]	ROE (%)	Related (REL) or Unrelated (UNRL)	Developed (DEV) or Bought (BT)	Transfers: Personnel (PER) or None (NO)	Control and Strategy: Integrated (INT) or Financial (FIN)
TW: Hilton	28	REL	BT	(NO)	(FIN)
Tiger: Leasing	18	UNRL	BT	PER	FIN
BR: Airline	16	—	—	—	—
WA: Airline	16	—	—	—	—
DL: Airline	15	—	—	—	—
TW: Canteen	15	UNRL	BT	(NO)	FIN
Tiger: Insurance	14	UNRL	BT	NO	FIN
Tiger: Airline	12	—	—	—	—
PA: Intercontinental	11	REL	DEV	(NO)	(FIN)
UAL: Airline	9	—	—	—	—
CO: Airline	9	—	—	—	—
NA: Airline	9	—	—	—	—
NW: Airline	8	—	—	—	—
UAL: Westin	8	REL	BT	Reverse	FIN
AA: Airline	5	—	—	—	—

AA: Subsidiaries	4[b]	REL	DEV	PER	INT
UAL: GAB Business Services	1	UNRL	BT	PER	FIN
BR: Educational Systems	(0)	REL	DEV	—[c]	FIN
EA: Airline	(1)	—	—	—	—
TW: Airline	(3)	—	—	—	—
PA: Airline	(7)	—	—	—[c]	—
BR: Hotels	(21)	REL	DEV	NO	INT
EA: Hotels	(35)	REL	DEV	NO	INT
EA: Distribution	(37)	UNRL	DEV		FIN
AA: Oil and gas	—[b]	UNRL	BT	PER	FIN
CO: Hotels	—[c]	REL	DEV	—[c]	INT
PA: Contract services	—[b]	REL	DEV	(PER)	(FIN)

Source: All numerical data derived from SEC reports; all classification data from interviews, reports, and literature. Some figures were adjusted for comparability.

Note: Notations in parentheses derived from secondary sources of information. Data in parentheses indicate losses.

[a] AA = American Airlines; BR = Braniff; CO = Continental; DL = Delta; EA = Eastern; FT = Flying Tiger; NA = National; NW = Northwest; PA = Pan American; TW = Trans World; UA = United Air Lines; WA = Western Airlines.

[b] Not meaningful; American's subsidiaries figure includes substantial business done with American; Pan American's contract services figures are not broken out.

[c] Unknown.

hence, this business will not be included in this analysis.) Braniff's hotel and education subsidiaries both had poor ROEs. Eastern's two ventures, hotels and National Distribution Services, were poor performers. Although it was not possible to compute a mean ROE for Continental's hotel venture, it incurred substantial losses; hence, a substantial negative ROE can be assumed.

Table 7–2, which covers the 1979–1983 period, is striking in two respects. First, it dramatically illustrates the potential that a well-implemented diversification program has to enhance corporate earnings. Second, it shows that, by 1979, most poorly-implemented diversification ventures were dropped and that, unfortunately, several profitable ventures had to be sold to finance airline losses (see chapter 5). Three new ventures were added in the 1977–1983 period: Trans World's Century 21 and Spartan Food Systems and Tiger's trucking ventures. The mean ROE series breaks naturally at about 7 percent, with all diversification ventures except Tiger's truck operations substantially outperforming all of the airlines, except (marginally) Delta.

Only one variable explains nearly all of these profitability differences. The ventures in the high-performance group were almost uniformly strong, ongoing firms when they were purchased. Hilton, Canteen, Century 21, Spartan, North American Car, Investors Mortgage Insurance, and Western International Hotels all fit into this category. Pan American's Intercontinental Hotels chain and contract services seem to be exceptions, but by this time they were so old and well-established that they can be considered to be in this category as well. GAB Business Services was basically a sound firm that had been run down for several years.

In contrast, all but one of the weak-performing ventures were developed internally by the airlines. Americana Hotels was put together by American, although one package of four hotels was purchased in a block from Loew's Hotels. Braniff's hotel chain and education ventures were put together by the airline. Although Rockresorts managed Eastern's individual hotels, the airline made key developmental decisions, such as which hotels to put together into a chain. National Distribution Services was also developed by Eastern. Continental's hotel chain was developed by the airline. Tiger's problematic trucking operation is the only exception; it will be analyzed later in the chapter.

Seen in this light, the relatedness of the diversification venture to the airline business can be a source of weakness rather than strength. The executives interviewed all perceived, for example, that the hotel business was related to the airline business. This perception at first glance seems to make sense; there are operational similarities in that both businesses require managing a labor-intensive, often seasonal operation. In addition, the markets are similar, because those who stay in hotels often fly to them.

Table 7–2
Comparison of Businesses along Several Dimensions, 1979–1983

Business[a]	ROE (%)	Related (REL) or Unrelated (UNRL)	Developed (DEV) or Bought (BT)	Transfers: Personnel (PER) or None (NO)	Control and Strategy: Integrated (INT) or Financial (FIN)
TW: Century 21	34	UNRL	BT	(NO)	FIN
TW: Hilton	31	–	–	–	–
TW: Spartan	27	UNRL	BT	(NO)	FIN
Tiger: Leasing[b]	25	–	–	–	–
PA: Intercontinental[b]	19	–	–	–	–
AA: Subsidiaries	17[c]	–	–	–	–
UAL: Westin	16	–	–	–	–
Tiger: Insurance[b]	14	–	–	–	–
TW: Canteen	11	–	–	–	–
UAL: GAB Business Services	7	–	–	–	–
DL: Airline	7	–	–	–	–
NW: Airline	3	–	–	–	–
AA: Airline	2	–	–	–	–

Table 7–2
Continued

Business[a]	ROE (%)	Related (REL) or Unrelated (UNRL)	Developed (DEV) or Bought (BT)	Transfers: Personnel (PER) or Skills (SK)	Control and Strategy: Integrated (INT) or Financial (FIN)
UAL: Airline	(2)	—	—	—	—
TW: Airline	(8)	—	—	—	—
EA: Airline	(29)	—	—	—	—
Tiger: Airline	(29)	—	—	—	—
PA: Airline	(30)	—	—	—	—
Tiger: Trucks	(31)	REL	BT	(NO)	(FIN)
WA: Airline	(35)	—	—	—	—
BR: Airline	Bankrupt	—	—	—	—
CO: Airline	Bankrupt	—	—	—	—
PA: Contract services	Strong[d]	—	—	—	—

Source: All numerical data derived from SEC reports; all classification data from interviews, reports, and literature. Some figures were adjusted for comparability.

Note: Notations in parentheses derived from secondary sources of information. Data in parentheses indicate losses.

[a] AA = American Airlines; BR = Braniff; CO = Continental; DL = Delta; EA = Eastern; FT = Flying Tiger; NA = National; NW = Northwest; PA = Pan American; TW = Trans World; UA = United Air Lines; WA = Western Airlines.

[b] Divested.

[c] Not meaningful; American's subsidiaries figure includes substantial business done with American; Pan American's contract services figures are not broken out.

[d] Exact figure not available.

Harry Mullikin, president and chief executive officer of Westin Hotels (formerly Western International Hotels), explained that the hotel business is related and similar to the airline business because it involves travel and people and is operated twenty-four hours a day. Also, both businesses produce services, and their advertising, sales, and promotion are similar.[2] As Rexford Bruno, former senior vice-president of the UAL, put it, both hotels and airplanes "need repeat customers and full houses."[3] Yet relatedness in itself does not explain why the hotel ventures of Trans World, UAL, and Pan American prospered, while those of American, Braniff, Eastern and Continental suffered.

Ironically, the difference between the two sets of hotel ventures is that the successful ventures were treated as independent, unrelated businesses by the holding company or airline management, whereas the unsuccessful ventures were run as related businesses, with strategies closely tied to the respective airlines. All key personnel interviewed at UAL agreed, for example, that the airline and hotel subsidiaries were operated independently. Mr. Bruno noted that UAL realized that it did not *need* hotels in the cities it served.[4] Mr. Mullikin stated that Westin's growth and development is guided by what is "best for" Westin; he believed that this was also good for UAL. Westin made no attempts to put hotels where they might be needed by United.[5] Also, Westin was run by managers with long-standing careers in the hotel industry.

The hotel subsidiary benefited from few exchanges of personnel or technology with United, the chief exception being computer reservations assistance. United benefited from substantial assistance from hotel personnel, however. Edward E. Carlson, former chairman of Western International Hotels, became chairman of UAL and United. He introduced significant innovations from the hotel industry, such as decentralized management and ongoing renovation of facilities. Westin was controlled mostly by monitoring return on investment and growth.[6]

Lynn P. Himmelman, former chairman of the executive committee of Western International Hotels and one of the deans of the U.S. hotel industry, observed similarities to his firm's relationship with UAL in the relationships between Trans World and Hilton and between Pan American and Intercontinental. He observed that Pan American was very successful in the hotel business, with good hotels in good markets, all properly financed. For many years, Pan American had hotel people running Intercontinental. He also noted that Hilton International has done a good job for Trans World. Hotel people ran the chain; like himself, the two heads of Hilton International were Cornell Hotel School graduates. Thus Westin, Hilton International, and Intercontinental have in common that they are solid, ongoing firms run with independence by managers with long careers in the hotel industry.[7] It is important that Pan American's cutting the hotel chain loose from airline management probably explains, to a large degree, its anomalous success.

The rather unsuccessful hotel ventures of American, Braniff, Eastern, and Continental have in common that they were developed by the respective airlines and that many crucial development decisions were made by airline managers who were inexperienced in hotel management. Albert Casey, current chairman of American, who took over American after Americana had largely been developed, provided a graphic illustration of this. He noted that the hotel chain, which had been largely sited in cities served by American or at resort locations coveted by American, was composed of diverse units and was not really a chain. He noted that Hilton and other chains had a pass-along capability via their reservations systems but that Americana's hotels did not have this characteristic because they were dissimilar in several important ways. The Americana in New York, for example, had 2,000 rooms and was primarily a convention hotel, while the Americana Aruba Hotel and Casino had 250 rooms and was a vacation resort. The second and fatal problem he noted was that many of the hotels were leased, not owned. He observed that the leases were negotiated by airline people (such as the former president of Americana) who were essentially amateurs in the hotel business. They fell into traps, such as agreeing to full payout leases without extensions or buyouts. Hence, many hotels carried burdensome leases and were extremely hard to divest. Third, Mr. Casey saw that because the hotels lacked commonality, a separate control and reservations system was required for each hotel. This made the hotels very hard for managers to manage.[8]

Braniff similarly ran into difficulty because it tied its hotels to the needs of the airline. One Braniff executive noted that moving from the airline to the hotel business was a "natural step." Braniff clearly saw hotels as an "addendum to the airline," and he noted that management was "airline-oriented." Braniff's hotel strategy was to "provide reasons for people to fly" to the airline's destinations, because there was not enough tourist infrastructure in South America. However, Braniff intended to make money on the hotels as well as in the airline traffic they were expected to generate.[9]

Continental and Eastern had similar problems. Continental sited hotels in Micronesia to gain routes and to develop traffic, but the hotel venture consistently lost money. Eastern acquired a hotel in Hawaii to gain routes and acquired one and developed one in Puerto Rico, which was served by the airline. Eastern's problems were similar to those of the other carriers in this group. The carrier management did not know the hotel business very well and approved hotels that a career hotel manager might not have approved. In fact, after Eastern turned the Mauna Kea in Hawaii back to Laurance Rockefeller, he expanded it and sold it to Westin, which ran it at a profit.[10]

Thus, the hotel ventures that were closely controlled and developed by the airlines made errors that seasoned hotel executives probably would not have made: most built at least some hotels that did not have enough business to break even; chains were developed without the basic commonalities they should have had; and leases were improperly negotiated. Perhaps the most common and fundamental error of this group was the assumption that the airline and hotels could cross-feed traffic. If the airline sited hotels in well-developed cities that were served by several carriers, competitive considerations in both industries generally precluded cross-feeding.[11] The weaknesses of the cross-feeding argument, mentioned in chapter 6, are relevant.

The two other related ventures, Braniff's Braniff Education Systems and Eastern's National Distribution Services, also fit with the explanation of performance developed here. Both were developed by airlines, and both performed poorly.

The history of National Distribution Services demonstrates the sorts of problems that chronically arose in internal development of ventures. National Distribution Services was set up to provide full warehouse services to small customers. By combining these firms' logistics operations under one roof, it was thought that sufficient scale could be gained to obtain joint economies and to carry a full range of services. Eastern expected to make some money from the sale of the system services, but primarily it expected the warehouse to stand completely on its own.[12]

Eastern had originally wanted the venture to be run by a particular distribution executive. After a lengthy negotiation process, however, it became clear that the individual would not take the position, so Eastern was stuck with the facilities in an advanced state of development and no president. It offered the position to a noted logistics expert who had little operating experience, and, unfortunately, he could not develop a staff and keep the project under control.[13] Faced with mounting losses, Eastern terminated the venture. These problems likely would not have arisen had Eastern acquired a solid, ongoing firm with a reservoir of competence in the business.

The unrelated ventures undertaken by the airlines were generally profitable. Tiger's two original nonairline subsidiaries, North American Car and Investors Mortgage Insurance, were outstanding performers. Both were stable, solid firms when they were acquired, and they were subsequently developed further by Tiger. UAL's GAB Business Services initially displayed a low mean ROE, but it built back from difficulties experienced under the former owners because there was a reservoir of expertise in the business. Trans World's Canteen acquisition and its more recent acquisitions of Century 21 and Spartan Food Systems brought it high returns. Thus, these six unrelated ventures had in common with the successful related ventures that they were purchased as solid firms with potential for development and that they were run independently.

It is important to make a distinction between airline development of new ventures, which has led to poor results, and marginal development of strong, ongoing acquired firms by transferred airline executives, which can lead to good results. There are two noteworthy instances of significant marginal improvements being wrought in an acquired firm by transferred airline executives: Tiger's Thomas Grojean's improvements to North American Car and UAL's Irvin Williamson's improvements to GAB Business Services. These two instances have two things in common. First, both firms had solid core structures and an ongoing competence in their respective industries. Second, both firms were embedded in rather inbred oligopolistic industries that rarely sought "new blood" from outside the industry.

After Tiger acquired North American Car (NAC), Thomas Grojean was sent in as president to revitalize the company. William Evans, Tiger's former comptroller, explained that NAC had previously been run very conservatively. At the beginning of each year, yearly quotas were set, such as "This year we will place X railroad cars costing Y." The quotas were determined simply by multiplying the change in retained earnings (with a 50 percent dividend) from the year before by a conservative leverage ratio. If this quota was met in, say, July, then NAC's management eased its efforts for the rest of the year (operations, of course, continued).[14]

Tiger's management felt that NAC did not have an adequate definition of its business and was not aggressive enough.[15] Thomas Grojean, then vice-president–finance of Tiger, wanted the top slot, and Tiger's chairman, Wayne Hoffman, agreed. Therefore, in 1971, Mr. Grojean was installed as president of NAC, and Martin Lynch, then Tiger's treasurer, was installed as NAC's vice-president–finance.[16]

The new management team made several changes. First, it filed amended tax returns and got back more than $15 million, which was a very substantial portion of the purchase price.[17] Second, Mr. Grojean changed the organization. Previously, everything had been stiff and hierarchical, with board approval required to justify every action. Mr. Grojean did everything directly. He recalled that everyone got enthused, and the change in attitude resulted in everyone becoming more upbeat and aggressive. He felt strongly that the top man has a tremendous influence on the lower-level people in a firm: "They should know that they will not get their heads bitten off if they make a mistake."[18]

Other changes were made in marketing, finance, and strategy. Mr. Grojean initiated a new marketing program, and Tiger backed it up with capital. Previously, NAC had been constrained to $60 million per year in asset purchases. This was necessary because the industry had previously paid large dividends amounting to 50 percent of earnings. Tiger immediately invested $25 million into NAC. It then cut out the dividend and leveraged this equity to the industry's traditional 4:1 debt-equity ratio. All later expansion came from internal sources, and all earnings were sheltered from taxes. NAC grew to over $700 million in asset purchases between 1971 and 1978.[19]

Under Mr. Grojean, NAC moved significantly into hopper cars and other specialized cars. Within four years, it ranked first in the industry in placement of new equipment. Previously, NAC had not built cars unless it had leases in hand. Tiger had it go long on cars, building without leases in hand. Mr. Grojean also altered the pricing structure. He cut prices, and others followed. Previously, NAC had charged less for long-term leases than for short-term leases. Mr. Grojean changed this to take inflation into account, and the rest of the industry followed his lead.[20]

Mr. Grojean continued to build and expand the business, acquiring firms to fill out his lines and moving into many countries. The important point here is that this is a case of an airline executive rendering significant improvements to an acquired ongoing business that probably would not have reached outside its industry for a new executive. Thus, here, airline diversification also led to substantial improvements in the acquired firm's industry, as NAC's competitors were forced to match Mr. Grojean's innovations. The turnaround in GAB Business Services shaped by UAL's Irvin Williamson also demonstrates this point.

Mr. Williamson was initially sent on a fact-finding mission to evaluate GAB. At that time, he was vice-president for finance of UAL, having been with UAL (or United) since 1966 and a partner in Arthur Andersen before that. After the acquisition, it became clear that important changes were needed in GAB. Mr. Williamson was made president of GAB and was given a mandate to make needed improvements.[21] These improvements were several. First, according to Mr. Williamson, as a new president he was able to change GAB's organization. The changes were not modeled after UAL's structure, but they probably could not have been made in this inbred industry had a major firm not taken over GAB, because an outsider could not have gotten in. Second, Mr. Williamson focused substantially increased attention on profit-center reporting, placing more emphasis on goal setting and more visible planning. He also installed an improved incentive compensation system. Third, with an initial assistance from UAL, Mr. Williamson greatly improved GAB's computer systems. When it was acquired, GAB had a seriously inadequate computer system and insufficient resources to improve it.

Mr. Williamson's reflections on how GAB benefited from its affiliation with UAL are apt. He noted that GAB derived benefits from being acquired by a large organization, because stability was introduced. After the company was divested by its original owners in 1973, it was clear to everyone that the venture capitalists who bought it were only short-term owners. The prospect of stability brought by UAL was particularly important to the work force.[22]

Mr. Williamson also noted that GAB was in a highly specialized business, and there were few managers with specific experience in the business. Hence, the management pool in the industry was very inbred. When UAL sent in Mr. Williamson as president, it introduced an outsider—hence, new ideas and skills. Mr. Williamson had no reluctance to commit funds, and, because of his ties with UAL, he had the ability to deliver funds.[23]

Mr. Williamson also noted that, even with its several initial problems, GAB was outperforming most of its competitors. He observed that after GAB upgraded its information-processing systems, its largest competitor overhauled its systems.[24]

Tiger presents the major apparent anomaly to the findings of this chapter: it purchased two strong, ongoing trucking companies, one of which performed poorly. The key to Tiger's problems was that the poorly performing larger firm, Hall's, even though it was in the relatively protected less-than truckload industry segment, was hard hit by the major changes (deregulation and recession) that followed. Warren, on the other hand, had a highly focused, protected niche, and it prospered (see Chapter 5). This suggests that the really crucial variable in predicting the success or failure of a diversifying venture is its intraindustry positioning and that strong, ongoing firms with seasoned, industry-specific managers tend to be well-positioned, whereas firms developed by those who are unfamiliar with the industry tend to be unfocused. In addition, a reservoir of industry-specific operating expertise is necessary to avoid naive errors. It is important to note that there is a big difference between running a single operating unit (such as one hotel) and developing a network that defines the company's strategic position (such as a hotel chain).

Evaluation

The single factor that explains the performance of the businesses into which the airlines diversified is the intraindustry competitive strategic position of the business. This is hardly surprising; it is consistent with the basic strategic framework given in this book. What is surprising, however, is that almost all of the businesses developed by the airlines experienced difficulties, whereas almost all of the businesses acquired as solid, ongoing firms with reservoirs of industry expertise prospered. Pan American's internal development of successful diversification was the exception that confirmed the rule: it had been developed over such a long period of time that it evolved into essentially independent entities that were well positioned in their industries. Tiger's purchase of a problematic truck line was also an exception that confirmed the rule: it acquired a solid, ongoing firm that was hurt by a major environmental change in its industry (much as deregulation hurt many airlines).

Seen in this light, the relatedness of a venture was more a handicap than a benefit. Airline managers were more likely to develop related businesses internally than to do so with unrelated businesses. Therefore, the related businesses were more likely to fail. (This does not mean that the airline managers were not competent in their own industry; rather, they were unfamiliar with the others.) This can be confirmed by observing the differences in control and integration of strategy among the businesses. Related businesses that were run independently (that is, as unrelated businesses) almost uniformly outperformed related ventures that were closely tied strategically and operationally to the respective airlines.

Transfers of personnel also were not generally determinants of profitability. When airline executives developed ventures from the start, poor results generally followed. Good results followed, however, when airline executives intervened in two strong, ongoing acquired firms (NAC and GAB). This had two likely causes: (1) these firms were in oligopolies with an inbred management pool, and acquisition was a key way to bring in fresh talent; and (2) the changes, though important, were marginal in the sense that they built on a reservoir of industry competence that was already present in a well-positioned firm. Importantly, the airlines frequently channeled resources from the airlines to the acquired ventures. This enabled many acquisitions to expand substantially and to build and consolidate their own intraindustry competitive positions.

It is relevant to note that the airline industry itself was traditionally a rather inbred oligopoly. The airlines benefited substantially from the periodic transfer of personnel from more competitive industries or segments. The two major successful reorganizations in the airline industry during the late regulated period were initiated by outsiders: Edward Carlson (and later Richard Ferris) of UAL was from Western International Hotels, and Albert Casey of American was from the Los Angeles Times-Mirror Company. More recently, American has prospered in deregulation under the presidency of Robert Crandall, who was also recruited from the outside. Pan American's C. Edward Acker and Texas International's Francisco Lorenzo have both imaginatively reorganized major carriers; both were from the entrepreneurial smaller-carrier segment of the industry. Although Northwest and Delta provide examples of solid, aggressive traditional airline management, the ancillary point remains that mixing aggressive managers from competitive industries into an inbred industry tends to bring benefits, and that diversification enhances this possibility.

Notes

1. This study has theoretical importance as well (see chapter 1 *supra,* note 14. By looking at performance differences among firms within an industry and at the performance of the diversification itself, problems of interindustry comparison can be avoided. Airlines have undertaken a variety of both related and unrelated ventures, and in each general category of diversification the ventures have exhibited a range of performance. This indicates that there is more to profitability than merely the relatedness of the ventures.

2. Mullikin interview (1979).
3. Bruno interview (1979).
4. Ibid.
5. Mullikin inteview (1979).
6. Ibid.
7. Himmelman interview (1979).
8. Casey interview (1979).
9. Background interview with a senior Braniff executive (1979).
10. Mullikin interview (1979).
11. Simons interview (1979).
12. Ibid.
13. Ibid.
14. Evans inteview (1979).
15. Hoffman interview (1979).
16. Grojean interview (1979).
17. Lynch interview (1979).
18. Grojean interview (1979).
19. Hoffman interview (1979).
20. Grojean interview (1979).
21. Williamson interview (1979).
22. Ibid.
23. Ibid.
24. Ibid.

8
Conclusion

This book has presented a systematic framework and procedure for managers of regulated and deregulated companies to use in developing corporate strategies for their firms. The strategic framework presented in chapter 1 provided a way for managers to relate their companies' intraindustry competitive situations to their corporate diversification possibilities both before and after deregulation. The essence of the strategic framework is that companies must look beyond the immediate competitive and operational problems in their traditional business; they also must constantly relate their long-run prospects in their traditional business to those available in others.

Regulation has a great impact on a regulated firm's prospects, as it influences each of the five forces that determine the firm's performance.[1] Where regulation systematically places a particular group of firms at a disadvantage, and they cannot jockey to improve their situation in that business, it becomes sensible for them to diversify until their returns equilibriate (unless this is barred by regulation). Deregulation lifts regulation's artificial influences on the five forces that determine a firm's prospects. It generally requires that firms shift toward competitive strategies that are appropriate for the industry's new underlying economic structure and its evolving competitive array. When a firm's prospects change, and its optimum size within its traditional business alters, its corporate diversification strategy should also adjust. In this way, the managers of a firm can link its intraindustry competitive strategy and its corporate diversification strategy to maintain value for their shareholders.

The strategic framework is relatively straightforward to articulate, but applying it to a particular industry requires careful attention to detail. The preceding chapters of this book have demonstrated its use by analyzing the airline industry over the past five decades. Currently, several other industries either are regulated or are in the process of being deregulated, including broadcasting, busing, financial services, moving, pipelines, public utilities, oil and gas, railroads, telecommunications, trucking, and water transport. Although there are important differences in the precise policies regulators have used and in the underlying economic structures of the industries, generalizations can be made to the extent that managers in all of these industries face the same analytical problems in the process of strategy formulation as well as many situational similarities. A manager in one firm must be very careful, however, not to simply observe and copy the successful strategies of other firms in the same industry or in other similar-looking industries. One must understand why an observed strategy was successful and be certain that the underlying conditions are sufficiently analogous to make the strategy appropriate in the situation at hand. Careful application of the strategic framework enables one to do this.

The first chapter of this book identified three specific sets of questions that are crucial to managers of regulated and newly deregulated firms:

1. What is an appropriate corporate strategy for a regulated firm, and when is it advantageous to diversify?
2. How can firms best manage the transition into deregulation, and what role should diversification play?
3. What determines the success or failure of diversification ventures?

The following sections of this chapter summarize and extend the answers to these questions and, finally, analyze the implications of these answers for society.

Corporate Strategy under Regulation

The most appropriate corporate strategy for a regulated firm can be determined by identifying its prospects within the regulated business and comparing them with those available in other businesses. The firm's long-term prospects in the regulated business depend on its position with respect to the particular regulatory policies prevailing in the industry, coupled with the industry's underlying economic structure and stage in its life cycle. When the basic regulatory policies in an industry turn systematically against particular firms, and they have exhausted all possibility of repositioning themselves or improving their efficiency within the industry, they should increase their diversification to raise their returns. Conversely, firms that benefit from these policies should retain or increase their focus on their traditional business. To understand and predict how and when regulation will systematically improve or hurt a firm's long-run, regulated-industry prospects, one must analyze how regulation is influencing each of the five forces that determine the firm's performance as the industry moves through its life cycle.

In the airline industry, the CAB's basic regulatory policies were developed when the industry was relatively young, and they remained relatively constant throughout the years. At the core of CAB regulation was cross-subsidy, a process through which price-insensitive buyers (passengers) and larger airlines supported marginal buyers and smaller airlines. To make cross-subsidy work, the CAB controlled price, restricted entry into the industry, and limited entry into and exit from particular segments of service. Labor, a politically powerful supplier, also benefited from cross-subsidy. These policies succeeded in nurturing the airline industry and expanding air travel in the industry's early years. With burgeoning demand, nearly all of the airlines prospered, and all remained essentially single-business firms.

As the industry began maturing in the early 1960s, however, growth slowed, and new customers became more price-sensitive. The larger airlines increasingly had to compete for each others' customers and jockey for regulatory favors to maintain their returns. As competition eroded their earnings on their prime routes, they were forced to continue cross-subsidizing both service on marginal routes and smaller airlines. This dramatically lowered their returns, both absolutely and relative to the smaller carriers' protected returns. The large carriers' response came in two stages. Initially, all large carriers (American, Eastern, Trans World, and United) and two smaller carriers (Braniff and Continental) undertook Type I diversification, siting hotels in an attempt to gain desirable routes. Ironically, this represented a basic commitment to the airline industry. When hotel siting failed to improve their long-run prospects, the large carriers systematically undertook a series of Type II diversification ventures. This represented a fundamental shift in corporate strategy; it was a deployment of resources outside the industry. The movement reflected the fact that the regulatory policies that had nurtured the industry in its early years became increasingly inappropriate as the industry changed and matured. Although this diversification pattern was influenced by a few secondary strategic goals, it was largely a sensible response by a group of firms to an environment that was increasingly unfavorable (relative to their competitors). It was entirely consistent with the prescriptions of the strategic framework developed in chapter 1.

Although there are differences among the regulatory policies in the various regulated industries, there are many important similarities. (For completeness, this section includes the experiences both of currently regulated industries and of currently deregulated industries when they were regulated.) Cross-subsidy, in various forms, has occurred in most regulated industries. In telecommunications, for example, long-distance service has cross-subsidized local service, business service has cross-subsidized residential service, urban service has cross-subsidized rural service, and brief calls have cross-subsidized lengthy calls. In trucking, dense line-haul service has cross-subsidized marginal rural service, and smaller firms have been kept in business partially by regulatory policies that split primary and back-haul authorities among different carriers. In the railroad industry, dense line-haul service has cross-subsidized marginal rural service, and several rate-splitting policies have helped the small branch lines. In intercity busing, dense line-haul services have cross-subsidized marginal rural services; and in public utilities, business service has cross-subsidized residential service.

Most regulatory agencies also have maintained barriers to entry into their respective industries, barriers to mobility into particular segments, and barriers to exit from particular services—much as the CAB did. The telecommunication industry, for example, long had barriers protecting both local services and long-distance service. The public utility industry has geographic barriers at the retail level. Both industry and geographic barriers have been common in financial services regulation. Certification, route entry, and route abandonment barriers were common to most transportation regulation. These barriers, and others like them in other industries, enabled regulators to prevent new entrants from picking off the high-priced services from which cross-subsidies were drawn.

Buyer power in most regulated industries was determined more by political influence than by intrinsic economic bargaining power. The substantial amount of cross-subsidy gives evidence of this. Similarly, supplier power in most regulated industries rested upon a political rather than an intrinsically economic basis; for example, labor unions in the rail, trucking, bus, and maritime industries routinely benefited from large settlements that were passed through to price-insensitive customers. In a parallel manner, Western Electric employees benefited in earlier years from generous policies whose costs were passed along to the ultimate customers. Finally, in several regulated industries, substitutes were regulated as well; for example, trucks were originally regulated to protect the railroad industry rate structure.

Interfirm rivalry has varied from industry to industry, but service and capacity competition generally took the place of price competition, much as it did in the airline industry.[2] Service and capacity competition included too many local bank branches (relative to the number that would have existed in a price-competitive industry), excessive securities industry research, and small appliance giveaways in the financial services industry, gasoline station contests in the oil industry, "piano bar wars" in the airlines, and merchandise discounts in telecommunications. Competition along these nonprice dimensions was less harmful to the firms than direct price competition.

The net effect of the regulatory policies on the prospects of particular firms or groups of firms within the various industries under regulation also varied widely. A firm's prospects depended on the specific application of the regulatory policies and on the industry's stage of development and underlying economic structure. In the airline industry, for example, interfirm cross-subsidy coupled with industry maturity to create systematic differentials between the returns of the smaller and the larger firms. In the public utility industry, increasing unit costs and stable demand systematically reversed the prospects of many firms.[3] In the telecommunications industry, major changes in technology turned the tide against the incumbents. Although a different set of firms was disadvantaged in each of these cases, managers in each of these industries' firms could use the same analytical procedure, described earlier, of tracing through the effects of regulation on the five forces in their respective industries to determine their firms' long-term prospects in their regulated businesses. Once the managers have analyzed these prospects and have convinced themselves that their firms have exhausted their possibilities for repositioning themselves, or improving their efficiency in their regulated industry, they can compare their firms' regulated business prospects to those available in other businesses and develop corporate diversification policies that maximize long-run returns. By applying this procedure, managers in regulated firms can formulate appropriate corporate strategies for their firms.

Corporate Strategy under Deregulation

In a deregulated industry, firms face many of the same intraindustry competitive positioning problems and corporate diversification possibilities as do firms in any competitive industry. The appropriate competitive strategy for any firm depends on its strengths and resources, the positioning of its competitors, and the industry's underlying economic structure and stage of development. Because regulation creates a largely artificial environment, most newly deregulated firms will not be well positioned for a competitive environment. Most will have to alter their intraindustry competitive strategies fundamentally so that they rest upon strengths appropriate for the new environment. Where deregulation diminishes a firm's prospects (either absolutely or relative to its competitors) in the regulated industry or force it to downsize into a defensible niche, the firm should increase its diversification with excess resources. On the other hand, if deregulation opens new opportunities for lucrative growth, or if impending price wars require additional resources, a firm should draw resources from its diversification to support its newly deregulated business. At the same time, an incumbent firm's transition from regulation to deregulation is generally slowed by transitory factors that can give new entrants a temporary but important edge.

Deregulation brought substantial changes to the airline industry. Regulatory barriers to entry and mobility were lifted, buyers' and suppliers' power reverted to an economic basis, cross-subsidy was eliminated, and price competition largely replaced service and capacity contests. In the newly deregulated industry, airlines had to create defensible and viable competitive strategies. They could aim at broad market-leadership strategies or focused niche strategies. A broad cost-leadership strategy was difficult to defend in the long run, because economies of scale were rather limited in the business. A broad-market, quality-service strategy was seen to offer in its differentiated product a potentially strong long-run position, once the new entrants' sizable but temporary cost advantage diminished. A focused, low-cost strategy centered on dense linear routes was seen to be the natural entry point for small, nonunion, new entrants and hence was not particularly defensible in the long run. A variety of other focused niche strategies were seen to offer the best prospect of long-run returns for the majority of the airlines. Carriers in this group could develop geographically focused, hub-based or gateway feeder strategies, or they could focus on particular segments of passengers to differentiate themselves from one another.

The strong, large airlines (United, American, and Delta) saw their prospects improve with deregulation. They sensibly focused on their airline businesses and drew on their diversification (as needed and available) for resources. Two of the weak, large carriers (Pan American and Eastern) tried to broaden their service and ran into trouble. They might better have focused on defensible and lucrative, but more limited, geographic niches built around their profitable services (much as Pan American did later) and used freed-up resources to strengthen their balance sheets and to diversify further. A third weak, large carrier (Trans World) achieved value for its shareholders by slowly downsizing its airline into a defensible niche, increasing its diversification, and ultimately spinning off the airline.

The strong, small airlines (Northwest and Braniff) pursued dramatically different strategies and achieved dramatically different results. Northwest earned substantial returns by steadily expanding its niche; with bright prospects in the airline industry, it had no need to diversify. In contrast, Braniff curtailed its diversification and sprinted toward a wide-service, market-leadership strategy. Without the resources to develop a host of new markets in a competitive environment, it rapidly went bankrupt. Two of the weak, small airlines (Continental and Western) continued to operate with route structures that were ideal under regulation but indefensible under deregulation, and both encountered severe problems. They might better have attempted to reposition themselves into defensible niches (as their new management teams later did); failing that, they might have fully diversified and exited the industry. The third weak, small airline (National) essentially did just that when it was acquired by Pan American; its dominant shareholders received substantial value, which could be reinvested into other businesses.

The airlines that experienced problems ran into trouble in two areas: they did not recast their airline strategies to make them defensible in terms of the industry's underlying economic structure, and they did not utilize diversification to ease the transition into deregulation. In contrast, the successful airlines created defensible airline competitive strategies that were appropriate for the new environment and matched them with corporate diversification strategies that reflected new equilibria among their respective prospects in the airline and alternative industries. At the same time, four temporary but important factors slowed the incumbents' strategic adjustment: several had to adjust the composition of their fleets; most had high labor costs and entrenched unions; many had difficulties acquiring the gates needed for route restructuring; and several had management teams that were oriented neither toward competing in a free market nor toward diversifying to build value for their shareholders. Though transient, these factors provided new entrants with a foothold in the market and gravely injured several established carriers.

Because each deregulated industry has a unique underlying economic structure and array of competitors, each must be analyzed separately to deduce the most sensible intraindustry competitive and corporate diversification strategies for particular firms. The analytical procedure is the same, however, from industry to industry; it rests upon use of the strategic framework developed in chapter 1, just as airline deregulation was analyzed in chapter 5.

The first step in deducing strategy for a deregulated firm is to untangle the effects of regulation and to analyze the industry's underlying economic structure.[4] This is best done by considering, in turn, each of the five forces that determine a firm's performance. The underlying economic structure varies widely from industry to industry; for example, whereas there are rather limited economies of scale (except in terminal operations and marketing) in the airline, trucking, and bus industries, there are marked economies of scale in telecommunications, railroads, and public utilities. This implies that the impact of large-scale operations on cost and market share is dramatically different for firms in these two sets of industries. As another example, whereas the airline, financial services, and trucking industries have differentiable products, the products of the long-distance segment of the telecommunications industry, the public utilities industry, and the gas transmission industry are much more like commodities and are therefore less differentiable. This implies that one set of firms can build differentiation-based entry barriers much more easily than the others. Similarly, the absolute capital barriers in several industries are substantially greater than those in others. Again, this has a great impact on the ability of firms to earn high returns behind entry barriers. Using this procedure, it is a detailed but tractable task to analyze each of the other forces that will determine the performance of firms in a deregulated industry. This analysis gives managers a basis for defining the set of defensible strategies for their firms that will rest upon real economic strengths in the deregulated industry.

Most new, low-cost entrants enter a regulated industry by "skimming the cream"—that is, targeting the price-insensitive, high-density services from which cross-subsidy was drawn under regulation. Long-distance business calls between New York and Washington, air travel between New York and Chicago, and line-haul, truckload trucking service on key high-density routes provide examples. Thus, established firms must be cautious about seizing these traditionally (under regulation) coveted services.

After laying out the set of strategies that will be feasible in the deregulated industry, managers facing deregulation must identify the transient factors that can slow their firms' transition and give new competitors an edge. In several industries, strong, entrenched unions have kept incumbents' costs high; this has led to bitter strikes in the bus, airline, and trucking industries. In other industries, firms have found themselves with inappropriate equipment; this problem has ranged from the airlines' surplus of long-haul equipment to ATT's difficulties in competing on price because its costly older equipment yielded high average-cost-based prices. In still other industries, buyers and smaller firms with entrenched political power slowed abandonment and price flexibility, as illustrated by delayed assessment of long-distance telephone access fees and slow phasing-out of airline price controls and route abandonment. Examples abound of regulated company management teams having substantial problems adjusting to the strategic positioning and operating problems of free competition. These examples merely represent the wide variety of temporary but important problems that can arise in a particular industry as it moves into deregulation. Managers must look at the factors in their own industry to determine if any will block their firms' transition toward any of the long-run strategies that appear to be feasible and defensible under deregulation. A firm's management must ensure that it does not get closed out or severely drained of resources trying to get to its target position.

The third step in strategy formulation for a company facing deregulation is to assess its own resources and position, both within its formerly regulated business and in other businesses into which it may have diversified. It is important to provide for ample resources for the transition period, as price competition is common while the firms in a deregulated industry reposition themselves into more defensible and stable postures. The orientation and value system of a firm's management must also be explicitly considered.

Once the managers of a particular firm understand its position, they should determine its existing and potential competitors' positions and project the strategies they will likely follow. Not only must a sensible strategy rest upon strengths appropriate for the new environment, but there must not be more firms than the market can support pursuing the strategy. For example, more airlines attempted wide-market, quality-service strategies than the market probably was capable of supporting; even though in isolation this was a basically sound competitive strategy, the weaker airlines in this group (e.g., Eastern and Trans World) faced problems.

A strategic map is a useful tool for laying out an industry's competitive array before deregulation and its likely competitive array after deregulation. In one particularly useful configuration, a low-cost versus quality-service orientation can be laid out on the horizontal axis, and a wide-market versus focused-niche scope can be laid out on the vertical axis.[5]

The preceding steps of analysis will enable a firm's management to choose a defensible intraindustry competitive strategy. At that point, the firm must size up both the amount of resources needed to implement the strategy and its long-run prospects in its deregulated as well as alternative businesses. Having done this, the firm can alter its corporate diversification strategy, if necessary, toward one that will enable it to maximize its long-run returns. By using this comprehensive analytical procedure, managers in deregulated firms in diverse industries can steer steady courses through apparent turmoil.

Diversification

For a firm to succeed, it not only must formulate a sensible strategy, it also must implement the strategy properly. The preceding two sections of this chapter concerned strategy formulation; this section concerns strategy implementation. The lessons of the airline experience are clear regarding the reasons for the success or failure of diversification ventures, and they are consistent with the basic thrust of the strategic framework at the heart of this book.

The ventures into which the airlines diversified displayed a wide range of profitability. The single variable that explained the performance of most of these cases was whether a business was developed internally by an airline or was acquired as a solid, ongoing firm with a reservoir of expertise in its industry. The underlying reason was found to be that the acquired firms were nearly always strong, ongoing enterprises that had seasoned, industry-experienced managers who had developed effective competitive strategies. Upon analysis, even the seeming exceptions, Pan American and Tiger, were seen to confirm this view.

Ironically, the more related a business was to the airline business, the more likely it was that airline managers would develop it themselves rather than buy it, and the more likely the business was to fail. (This does not mean that airline managers were not competent in their own business.) This was confirmed by observing that the related businesses that were run independently (as unrelated businesses) by seasoned, industry-specific operating executives almost uniformly outperformed those in the same industry that were closely tied strategically and operationally to the respective airlines. Most fatal diversified venture errors probably would not have been made by managers who were experienced in the acquired firms' industries. This was recognized after the fact by the airline executives involved.

The airline experience also suggests that a diversified firm should view its portfolio of businesses not only from a managerial point of view but also from an investment point of view. The markets for firms in various industries, and for the underlying assets of those firms, have ups and downs. Shrewd timing of the purchase and sale of businesses sometimes will yield as high returns as stellar management of the firms. American Airlines, for example, made up for substantial operating losses through the sale of the various hotels of its Americana chain, because its chairman, Albert Casey, sold them at the peak of a strong market, despite the fact that they posted mounting losses as a chain.

This study has also shown that several often-illusory reasons for diversification are frequently cited to justify such a move. It is important to review them so that a firm can avoid these traps. Synergism and joint economies were not observed in the study; in fact, substantial diseconomies were often found. Joint marketing and cross-feeding traffic were also illusory goals; more often than not, the fear of competitive retaliation precluded any gains of this type. Merging to gain tax shelters or earnings that might be sheltered was not a sound strategy; the tax situation of a firm could be managed better through the lease versus buy decision for capital assets. In sum, when it is carefully thought through and sensibly done, diversification can be a very powerful strategic tool for managers in an evolving dynamic economy.

Implications for Society

Regulation has had, and continues to have, an important role to play in the development of our economy. It can help harness natural monopolies, foster new industries, and protect the public safety and environment. Yet there are situations in which regulation can be counterproductive, as sections of this book have graphically illustrated. Against this background, many public policymakers have asked whether regulated industry diversification is good for society. While one must be careful not to simply generalize from an analysis of one industry, this study has provided a framework to enable policymakers to analyze other industries. Moreover, this book's analysis of the airline industry's experience suggests several lessons that should be crucial components in public policy debates in other industries.

The underlying regulatory problem in the airline industry, as developed in the early chapters of this book, was that the industry changed over time, while the CAB's regulatory policies remained relatively static. The CAB, as a regulatory body, tended to take on a life of its own: it developed momentum and its policies developed inertia. This caused the regulatory policies in force to diverge over time from those that would have been appropriate for the evolving airline industry. This divergence played a major role in causing the airline industry's problems from 1960 through its recent deregulation, with its convoluted dynamic in which the strongest firms systematically disinvested, and the inefficient firms were kept in business.

In this context, was regulated airline diversification good for society? The answer on balance is positive. Well-implemented diversification provided an outlet for several airlines, a renewal and recycling of resources to more productive and desired uses, and a way to move away from stale, unrenumerative situations. Under regulation, airline diversification acted as a barometer: it provided a way to relate regulation to the real, evolving situation in the industry. When the group of strong airlines was systematically diversifying out of the industry, it was a solid indication that there was a problem with the regulation. To the extent that other regulatory agencies' policies diverge over time (unless extraordinary and painful efforts are taken) from those that would be appropriate for the evolving regulated industries, the airline experience offers valuable lessons.

Balancing the social benefits of diversification were some problems. As with any strategy, poorly implemented diversification at times led to poor results; and poor results provided the basis for dramatic "war stories" and for legitimate concerns that diversification would divert corporate management attention and resources away from improving the efficiency of the regulated business—to the public's detriment. However, the positive role that diversification can play in a regulated industry should not be obsured by problems in putting the strategy into practice. As chapter 7 has demonstrated, diversification has played a major role in keeping several airlines solvent in recent years. The important lesson of chapter 7 is that practice can be improved by systematic analysis of actual experience; improvement rather than elimination of the strategy or arbitrary measures such as restricting diversification to a maximum percentage of the total corporate revenues or resources, is the best way to bring about good results.

This leads to a final question: Was diversification of deregulated airlines good for society? Again, the answer on balance is positive. Chapter 5 showed how well-implemented diversification could enable a deregulated firm to reposition itself into a more defensible stance. Again, as with any strategy, implementation problems can lead to poor results. But the airline experience suggests that those concerned work to improve practice by careful analysis, rather than by arbitrarily restricting or prohibiting diversification.

Over the long run, in a deregulated industry, as well as in a freely competitive industry, diversification can play an important role in the industry's life cycle: it can offer an alternative to reinvestment when capacity is in surplus, and it can enable firms that are unable to maneuver into an advantageous competive posture to exit from the industry. Yet poorly conceived diversification has the potential to distract managers from the important tasks of improving their firms' efficiency and competitive positioning; and poorly managed diversification has the potential to squander valuable resources. The key is good management grounded in good analysis. Well-managed diversification can play a vital role in enabling an economy to remain resilient, and in keeping resources productively employed. In this way, managers who carefully develop sound corporate strategies that benefit their stockholders can benefit society as well.

Notes

1. The five forces identified by Porter (1980) as determining the performance of a firm are the threat of new entrants, buyer bargaining power, supplier bargaining power, the threat of substitutes, and rivalry among existing firms (see chapter 1 *supra*).

2. See Fruhan (1972) and Meyer (1983).

3. See Thompson (1984).

4. Porter (1980) gives a detailed analysis of the formulation of competitive strategy in light of a firm's underlying industry economic structure.

5. See Porter (1980). Meyer (1983) gives several examples of this procedure.

Appendix A:
An Analysis of the Air Carrier
Reorganization Investigation

B oth the Civil Aeronautics Board (CAB) and the Interstate Commerce Commission (ICC) were concerned with diversification of transportation carriers in the late 1960s and early 1970s. In keeping with their legislative charge to protect the shipping public, they sought to institute measures to ensure that carrier diversification did not cause service to erode. Their concern was focused by a suspicion that the spectacular Penn Central bankruptcy was caused, in large part, by the company's siphoning railroad assets into a diversionary diversification program, thus crippling the carrier and endangering the shipping public. The ICC and the Congress conducted a series of investigations and hearings on the issue from the late 1960s through the mid-1970s. They found several possible incidents of rail carrier diversion of rail assets into other businesses that the ICC was powerless to regulate.[1]

Concurrent with this development, and in large part because of the same concerns, the CAB held a lengthy investigation of air carrier diversification, entitled Air Carrier Reorganization Investigation (Docket 24283). In brief, this investigation, which lasted from 1971 through 1975, was triggered by Braniff's request to reorganize into a holding company for the purpose of diversification. The investigation also examined the corporate structures of UAL, Inc. (the parent of United Air Lines), and Flying Tiger, Inc. (the parent of Flying Tiger Lines), both of which had diversified significantly since reorganizing into a holding company form. The basic finding of the investigation was that although diversification could conceivably benefit a firm overall, protections were necessary to ensure that the carriers did not excessively divert carrier resources to other businesses and fail to serve the public interest.

Although some diversification had taken place in the air carrier industry, until the late 1960s, the air carriers were parent companies to the diversified subsidiaries, so the entire companies remained subject to CAB regulation. This changed, however, in 1970, when United Air Lines reorganized into a subsidiary of a newly formed holding company, UAL, Inc., and acquired Western International Hotels. At the time, the CAB did not have jurisdiction to regulate the reorganization. In August 1969, the Congress amended Section 408 of the Federal Aviation Act of 1958 to give the CAB jurisdiction over such corporate reorganizations. In 1969, Flying Tiger Lines reorganized into a subsidiary of a newly formed holding company, Flying Tiger, Inc., and in 1971 it acquired North American Car Company and National Equipment Rental. In 1971, Braniff applied to the CAB for permission to reorganize into a subsidiary of a newly formed holding company, Braniff International, and to spin off its hotel interests in South America into Braniff International Hotels, an affiliated subsidiary. All three carriers indicated that they intended to diversify further should appropriate opportunities present themselves, and that they would not feel constrained to remain in transportation-related fields.[2]

These actions prompted the CAB to conduct the Air Carrier Reorganization Investigation. The thrust of the inquiry was twofold; it was directed both to the desirability of diversification for air carriers in general and to the problem of how to ensure that the carrier subsidiary of a diversified holding company remained able to serve the public interest adequately.

Because most airlines were diversifying *de novo* and the industry was still attractive, the CAB noted that the focus of diversification was less on developing nontransportation assets, as railroads had been doing, and more on remedying particular problems of the airline industry. Among the problems cited were extreme cyclicality, regulatory blockage of growth, and relatively low earnings stemming from a combination of inflationary labor and fuel costs and extreme equipment and schedule competition.[3] Chief among the advantages of diversification cited by carriers were operating economies, better access to capital markets, lower cost of capital, economies due to production synergy, and economies due to joint purchasing.

Important among the potential problems noted by the CAB were possible financial manipulation by issuance of excessive dividends; removal of assets, such as tax credits or working capital; removal of assets and services to the parent or affiliate for less than fair market value; purchase of assets and services from the parent or affiliate for more than fair market value; and loading costs on the carrier through improper allocation of overheads or joint costs. The essence of these concerns was that by loading costs onto the airline, regulatory authorities would have to set higher rates; thus, the traveling public would pay the price for the diversification. Although these potential disadvantages might be detrimental to a carrier, they would not be detrimental to its stockholders. Possible antitrust problems that would be detrimental to society as a whole were raised, however, including predatory pricing, tying arrangements, and reciprocal buying.[4]

In discussing the advantages and disadvantages of diversification in light of the hearing record, the administrative law judge found that diversification could adversely affect a carrier if funds were channeled to more profitable affiliates rather than to the carrier. This would be particularly problematic where a holding company form of organization was used, rather than where the air carrier was the parent of diversified subsidiaries. The judge felt that the greatest protection for carrier interests rested in having the carrier dominate the firm. He reasoned that this would diminish the impact on the carrier of an unsuccessful diversification, and it would make it imperative to maintain a healthy carrier so that the returns of the whole firm remained healthy. Since other subsidiaries would be easier to acquire under a holding company form of organization, he found that organization as a carrier-parent with subsidiaries would be better for the carrier and for the public interest.[5]

The judge felt that diversification would tend to dampen the cyclicality of earnings in many cases, but, he stated, "all business activities tend to follow the same economic trends and, in any event, air carriers will not and should not acquire noncarrier businesses to the extent that would be needed to have substantial effects on the cyclicality of earnings." In addition, some complementarity was seen to be possible in short-term financing needs, and a role was seen for interaffiliate loans.[6]

Benefits in reducing the labor-intensity of firms were cited by the judge, particularly in the case of Flying Tiger, which acquired highly capital-intensive leasing businesses. This was seen to give them a hedge against cost increases in a major airline cost factor. The exposure of the firms to fuel cost inflation could be lowered in a like manner, with similarly beneficial results. Filing of consolidated tax returns was cited as enabling the firms to take advantage of unused tax shelters and investment tax credits, although investment tax credits could be recouped somewhat through leasing. Potential economies of scale, production synergy, and joint purchasing savings were, by carrier admission, not important or significant. The concern was raised that diversification might divert management's attention from its carrier, leading to less-efficient carrier operations.

In general, the examiner felt that none of the advantages would accrue specifically to the carriers; rather, they would accrue to the stockholders of the holding companies. Regarding the disadvantages, he found that if unrelated diversification were to take place, as well it might, it might lower the cost of equity, but the holding companies might choose not to reinvest in the carriers. Also, in hard times, working capital might not be returned to the carriers, as happened in the Penn Central case. Indeed, he saw Flying Tiger moving in that pattern. He reasoned that this could lower working capital to dangerous levels, impair the carriers' ability to finance fleet replacement, or make it impossible to defray the cost of adequate air transportation service. Antitrust problems were felt to be controllable with existing legislation and enforcement.

In devising a remedy to control potential abuses, the CAB took careful note of the important differences between railroads and airlines, as detailed in the Department of Transportation (DOT) brief, which noted that railroads are more capital-intensive than airlines. Significant railroad assets are in real estate, which can readily be turned into cash without any outward change in ownership and without necessarily impairing the transportation functions. Railroads can generate cash by deferring maintenance. In contrast, airlines' fixed assets are mostly in the form of flight equipment, which is highly visible when sold; hence, it is easier to detect disinvestment. Airlines also cannot defer maintenance, because they are bound by Federal Aviation Administration regulations. (They can, however, defer investment in new equipment.) Finally, airline rates of return have historically been substantially higher than railroad rates of return.[7]

These differences led the CAB to adopt a more flexible regulatory stance than that desired by the ICC for railroads. The CAB opted for monitored self-regulation. Carriers wishing to reorganize were required to submit for approval transaction agreements that specified in advance their policies covering dividends; management services provided for or by the carrier by or for a member of its affiliated group, including, but not limited to, accounting, legal, clerical, financial, and other administrative services; joint use of employee time; joint marketing; transfers of goods and services; purchasing or leasing; loans and advances between affiliates; real and personal noncash assets transfers; leases of property and equipment; joint use of assets and facilities; tax allocations; tour packages with affiliated hotels; and guarantees, pledges of stock or assets, compensating balances, security, or other credit support by the air carrier.[8]

The CAB concomitantly issued a set of transaction guidelines that set forth the minimum that would be acceptable in each category. It required quarterly transaction reports detailing interaffiliate and parent–subsidiary transactions in which a carrier was a party. In addition, prior information regarding acquisitions had to be filed, as did annual financial statements for each member of the corporate group.[9]

The third component of CAB regulation of diversification was to be a requirement that performance-monitoring reports be filed and kept current. Among the topics to be covered in these reports was a statement on allocation of funds among the members of the group, including short-term financing and contingency plans for carrier working capital in an earnings downturn. Also required was a current statement of dividend policy, including interaffiliate funds transfers. Finally, statements were required on the current status of debt restrictions and on provision for credit support and risks taken on behalf of affiliates. It is noteworthy that although most of the CAB regulatory framework aligns with the DOT proposals, the DOT sensibly suggested performance monitoring of direct measures, such as market share and consumer complaints, as indicators of performance. The CAB chose, instead, to monitor every transaction, rather than performance measures.[10]

In reviewing this decision, it is striking that no one raised the possibility that diversification could change the rules of the competitive game and thus bring airline returns into line with those prevailing in alternative investments in other sectors of the economy. This could be expected to lead carriers to decrease capacity until supply and demand equilibrated in various markets.[11] At that time, there would not be a need for artificial capacity agreements or complex rate-making formulae with standard load factors. (This assumes the arguments of Caves [1962] and others that the underlying industry structure was conducive to competition.) It is an understandable omission, however. The CAB was guarding against disinvestment, as it believed that higher fares and lower service levels would result. In any event, the decision was overturned in 1977 by the appeals court, which ruled in favor of United on the grounds that because these measures applied only to carriers that were subsidiaries of holding companies, they were illegal. Thus, the CAB lost its hope of regulating air carrier diversification, and carriers received a green light for further diversification.

Notes

1. See, for example, U.S. Senate, Committee on Commerce (1972). Also, U.S. Interstate Commerce Commission (1977) contains a history of regulatory hearings and recommendations.
2. See U.S. Civil Aeronautics Board (1973) and U.S. Department of Transportation (1973d).
3. Ibid.
4. Ibid.
5. Ibid.
6. Ibid.
7. See U.S. Department of Transportation (1973d).
8. See U.S. Civil Aeronautics Board (1973).
9. Ibid.
10. Ibid.
11. Fruhan (1972) develops this argument.

Bibliography

Books and Journal Articles

Andrews, K.R. *The Concept of Corporate Strategy.* Homewood, Ill.: Dow Jones–Irwin, 1980.

Averich, H., and Johnson, L.L. "Behavior of the Firm Under Regulatory Constraint." *American Economic Review,* December 1962.

Baumol, W.J. *Business Behavior, Value and Growth,* rev. ed. New York: Harcourt Brace, 1967.

Bower, J.L. *Managing the Resource Allocation Process.* Boston: Harvard Graduate School of Business Administration, Division of Research, 1970.

Byrnes, J.L.S. "Air Carrier Diversification." Unpublished doctoral dissertation, Harvard Graduate School of Business Administration, 1980.

Capron, W.M. (Ed.). *Technological Change in Regulated Industries.* Washington, D.C.: Brookings, 1971.

Caves, R.E. *Air Transport and Its Regulators.* Cambridge, Mass.: Harvard University Press, 1962.

Caves, R.E., and Porter, M.E. "From Entry Barriers to Mobility Barriers: Conjectural Decisions and Contrived Deference to New Competition." *Quarterly Journal of Economics,* May 1977.

Chandler, A.D., Jr. *Strategy and Structure: Chapters in the History of the American Industrial Enterprise.* Cambridge, Mass.: MIT Press, 1962.

———. *The Visible Hand: The Managerial Revolution in American Business.* Cambridge, Mass.: Belknap Press, Harvard University Press, 1977.

Channon, D.F. *The Strategy of British Enterprise.* Boston: Harvard Graduate School of Business Administration, Division of Research, 1973.

Christenson, C.R.; Andrews, K.R.; Bower, J.L.; Hammermesh, R.G.; and Porter, M.E. *Business Policy: Text and Cases.* Homewood, Ill.: Irwin, 1982.

Cohen, K.J., and Cyert, R.M. *Theory of the Firm: Resource Allocation in a Market Economy.* Englewood Cliffs, N.J.: Prentice-Hall, 1965.

Copeland, S. *The Story of Western International Hotels.* Seattle: Western International Hotels, 1976.

Cunningham, L.F., and Wood, W.R. "Diversification in Major U.S. Airlines." *Transportation Journal,* Spring 1984.

Daughen, J.R., and Binzen, P. *The Wreck of the Penn Central.* New York: Signet, 1973.

Davies, R.E.G. *A History of the World's Airlines.* London: Oxford University Press, 1967.

Fruhan, W.E. *The Fight for Competitive Advantage: A Study of the United States Domestic Trunk Air Carriers.* Boston: Harvard Graduate School of Business Administration, Division of Research, 1972.

Gort, M. *Diversification and Integration in American Industry.* Princeton: Princeton University Press, 1962.

———. "An Economic Disturbance Theory of Mergers." *Quarterly Journal of Economics,* November 1963.

Gort, M., and Hogarty, T.F. "New Evidence on Mergers." *Journal of Law and Economics,* April 1970.

Hindley, B., "Separation of Ownership and Control in the Modern Corporation." *Journal of Law and Economics,* April 1970.

Hogarty, T.F. "The Profitability of Corporate Mergers." *Journal of Business,* July 1970.

Johnson, R.E. *Airway One.* Chicago: R.R. Donnelley & Sons, 1974.

Kahn, A.E. *The Economics of Regulation.* New York: Wiley, 1970.

Kotler, P.J. *Marketing Management.* Englewood Cliffs, N.J.: Prentice-Hall, 1976.

Lawrence, P.R., and Lorsch, J.W. *Organization and Environment: Managing Differentiation and Integration,* Homewood, Ill.: Irwin, 1967.

Leibenstein, H. "Allocative Efficiency vs. X-Efficiency." *American Economic Review,* June 1966.

Lipsey, R.G., and Lancaster, K. "The General Theory of the Second Best." *Review of Economic Studies,* 1956.

Lorie, J.H., and Halperin, P. "Conglomerates: The Rhetoric and the Evidence." *Journal of Law and Economics,* April 1970.

Maister, D.H. "Technical and Organizational Change in a Regulated Industry: The Case of Canadian Grain Transport." In W.T. Stanbury (Ed.), *Studies on Regulation in Canada.* Montreal: Institute for Research on Public Policy, 1978.

Markham, J.W. *Conglomerate Enterprise and Public Policy.* Boston: Harvard Graduate School of Business Administration, Division of Research, 1973.

Meyer, J.R. "A Position Paper." In *Report of the Fifth Workshop on National Transportation Problems.* Washington, D.C.: U.S. Government Printing Office, 1976.

———. "Toward a Better Understanding of Deregulation: Some Hypotheses and Observations." *International Journal of Transport Economics,* April-August, 1983.

Meyer, J.R., and Oster, C.V., Jr. (Eds.). *Airline Deregulation: The Early Experience.* Boston: Auburn House, 1981.

———. (Eds.). *Deregulation and the New Airline Entrepreneurs,* Cambridge, Mass.: MIT Press, forthcoming-a.

———. (Eds.). *Airline Deregulation and the Future of Intercity Travel.* Cambridge, Mass.: MIT Press, forthcoming-b.

Meyer, J.R.; Peck, M.J.; Stenason, J.; and Zwick, C. *The Economics of Competition in the Transportation Industries.* Cambridge, Mass.: Harvard University Press, 1959.

Moody's Transportation Manual. New York: Moody's Investors Services, 1977, 1978, 1979.

Myers, S.C. *Modern Developments in Financial Management.* Hinsdale, Ill.: Dryden Press, 1976.

Porter, M.E. *Interbrand Choice, Strategy, and Bilateral Market Power.* Cambridge, Mass.: Harvard University Press, 1976.

————. "The Structure Within Industries and Company Performance." Working paper, Harvard Graduate School of Business Administration, Division of Research, September 1977.

————. *Competitive Strategy.* New York: Free Press, 1980.

Rhoades, S.A. "The Effect of Diversification on Industrial Profit Performance in 241 Manufacturing Industries: 1963." *Review of Economics and Statistics,* May 1973.

Rumelt, R.P. *Strategy, Structure and Economic Performance.* Boston: Harvard Graduate School of Business Administration, Division of Research, 1974.

Salter, M.S., and Weinhold, W.A. *Diversification Through Acquisition.* New York: Free Press, 1979.

Scott, B.R. "Stages of Corporate Development." Unpublished manuscript, Harvard Graduate School of Business Administration, 1971.

Sherer, F.M. *Industrial Market Structure and Economic Performance.* Chicago: Rand McNally, 1970.

Simon, H.A. *Administrative Behavior.* New York: Free Press, 1957.

Steiner, P.O. *Mergers: Motives, Effects, Policies.* Ann Arbor: University of Michigan Press, 1975.

Straszheim, M.R. *The International Airline Industry.* Washington, D.C.: Brookings, 1969.

Taneja, N.K. *The Commercial Airline Industry.* Lexington, Mass.: Lexington Books, D.C. Heath, 1976.

————. *The U.S. Airfreight Industry.* Lexington, Mass.: Lexington Books, D.C. Heath, 1979.

————. *Airlines in Transition.* Lexington, Mass.: Lexington Books, D.C. Heath, 1981.

Thompson, A.A., Jr. "The Electric Utility Industry in 1982." In *Strategic Management: Concepts and Cases.* Plano, Tex.: Business Publications, 1984.

U.S. Civil Aeronautics Board. *Air Carrier Reorganization Investigation: Decision of E. Robert Seaver, Administrative Law Judge (Docket 24283 et al.).* Washington, D.C.: U.S. Government Printing Office, 1973.

————. *Handbook of Airline Statistics.* Washington, D.C.: CAB, 1950–1984.

U.S. Department of Transportation. *Brief to Administrative Law Judge E. Robert Seaver on the Air Carrier Reorganization Investigation (Docket 24283 et al.).* Washington, D.C.: U.S. Government Printing Office, 1973a.

————. *Brief to the Civil Aeronautics Board for the Air Carrier Reorganization Investigation (Docket 24283 et al.).* Washington, D.C.: U.S. Government Printing Office, 1973b.

————. *Reply Brief to Administrative Law Judge E. Robert Seaver on the Air Carrier Reorganization Investigation (Docket 24283 et al.)* Washington, D.C.: U.S. Government Printing Office, 1973c.

————. *Study of Selected Railroad Holding Companies: Direct Exhibit 3 of Testi-*

mony before the Civil Aeronautics Board in the Air Carrier Reorganization
Investigation (Docket 24283 et al.) Washington, D.C.: U.S. Government Printing Office, 1973d.

U.S. Interstate Commerce Commission. *Railroad Conglomerates and Other Corporate Structures.* Washington, D.C.: U.S. Government Printing Office, 1977.

U.S. Senate, Committee on Commerce, Special Staff. *The Penn Central and Other
Railroads.* Washington, D.C.: U.S. Government Printing Office, 1972.

U.S. Senate, Committee on the Judiciary, Antitrust and Monopoly Subcommittee.
Economic Concentration Hearings, 91st Congress. Washington, D.C.: U.S.
Government Printing Office, 1969.

Van Horne, J.D. *Financial Management and Policy.* Englewood Cliffs, N.J. Prentice-
Hall, 1977.

Williamson, J.D. "Profit, Growth and Sales Maximization." *Econometrica,* February
1966.

Wyckoff, D.D., and Maister, D.H. *The Domestic Airline Industry.* Lexington,
Mass.: Lexington Books, D.C. Heath, 1977.

Interviews

Bruno, Rexford E., Senior Vice-President–Administration and Finance, UAL; interview of May 21, 1979.

Casey, Albert V., Chairman, American Airlines; interview of May 2, 1979.
———. letter of December 20, 1979.

Evans, William D., Comptroller, Tiger International; interview of June 5, 1979.

Goss, Jackson, President, Tiger Insurance; interview of June 25, 1979.

Grojean, Thomas, President, Tiger International; interview of June 7, 1979.

Himmelman, Lynn P., Chairman of the Executive Committee, Western International Hotels, and Director, UAL; interview of July 5, 1979.

Hoffman, Wayne, Chairman, Tiger International, interview of June 4, 1979.

Lynch, Martin, Vice President–Finance and Treasurer, Tiger International; interview of June 5, 1979.

Mullikin, Harry, President and Chief Executive Officer, Westin Hotels (formerly
Western International Hotels), and Director, UAL; interview of July 5, 1979.

Simons, Charles, Vice-Chairman and Executive Vice-President, Eastern Airlines;
interview of September 26, 1979.

Williamson, Irvin E., Chairman and Chief Executive Officer, GAB Business Services, interview of May 29, 1979.

Background interview with a senior Braniff executive, 1979.

Periodicals and Reports

Aviation Week and Space Technology: 6/3/68.
Business Week: 10/6/73, 6/29/74, 3/22/76, 3/19/84, 4/23/84, 6/11/84.
Forbes: 11/15/76.

Fortune: 6/13/83, 10/17/83, 6/11/84.
New York Times: 1/11/84, 2/26/84.
Various airline annual reports (denoted in text by the airline name and year)
Various airline SEC reports (denoted in text by the airline name and year)

Index

About the Author

Jonathan L.S. Byrnes received the M.B.A. from Columbia University and the D.B.A. from the Harvard Graduate School of Business Administration. In the past, he has served as a department head for a major U.S. transportation company, as a faculty member at Rensselaer Polytechnic Institute, and as editor-in-chief of *Columbia Journal of World Business*. He is currently an associate professor of business administration at Northeastern University, where he teaches courses in business policy and in transportation and logistics. In addition, he is a consultant to several major domestic and foreign corporations and governments.